AS FAITH MATURES

BEYOND THE SUNDAY GOD

Mary Beth Werdel, PhD

AS FAITH MATURES

BEYOND THE SUNDAY GOD

Mary Beth Werdel, PhD

Liguori
LIGUORI, MISSOURI

Imprimi Potest:
Harry Grile, CSsR, Provincial
Denver Province, The Redemptorists

Published by Liguori Publications
Liguori, Missouri 63057

To order, call 800-325-9521
www.liguori.org

Library of Congress Cataloging-in-Publication Data

Werdel, Mary Beth.
As faith matures : beyond the Sunday God / Mary Beth Werdel. —1st ed.
    p. cm.
ISBN 978-0-7648-2152-3
1. Spirituality—Catholic Church. 2. Spiritual life—Catholic Church.
I. Title.
BX2350.65.W47 2012
248.4'82—dc23

                                                                    2012029420

p ISBN 978-0-7648-2152-3

e ISBN 978-0-7648-2301-5

Liguori Publications, a nonprofit corporation, is an apostolate of The Redemptorists. To learn more about The Redemptorists, visit Redemptorists.com.

Printed in the United States of America
16 15 14 13 12 / 5 4 3 2 1
First Edition

For Matthew, my gift from God.

Contents

Acknowledgments

In my life I have been blessed with a number of role models who have encouraged me to spend time wondering about God and helped me come to both believe and feel that God wonders about me, too. It is with gratitude that I acknowledge Mary Nazzaro, Lucia Nazzaro, Anne Werdel, Daniel St. Laurent, Randy Schroeder, Mary Marguerite Kohn, Crescentia Healy True, Crescentia Anne Healy, Eryn True, Emma True, Peter Werdel, and William Werdel for encouraging and supporting the maturation of my faith. As well, Robert J. Wicks, my mentor and my friend, encouraged and guided me throughout the process of writing this book, from the very first word to the very last. I am deeply grateful for his persistent encouragement to live and write well. Finally, this book would have remained merely a passing thought in my mind if not for the support of Christy Hicks, editor at Liguori Publications. I am thankful for Christy's belief in this project; I am thankful for her belief in me.

About the Author

Dr. Mary Beth Werdel is an assistant professor of pastoral care and counseling in the Graduate School of Religion and Religious Education at Fordham University. She earned her doctorate from Loyola University Maryland. She has both a master's degree in counseling and a bachelor's degree in English from the University of New Hampshire. She writes and lectures on the relationships found in spirituality, trauma, and growth. She is co-author of the book *A Primer on Posttraumatic Growth: An Introduction and Guide* (2012) published by Wiley. She is also published in the journals *Research in the Social Scientific Study of Religion, Alcohol Treatment Quarterly*, and *Human Development*. Dr. Werdel is a licensed professional counselor and most recently worked as a family therapist with primarily Spanish-speaking immigrant families from El Salvador and Mexico. She has traveled extensively in Central America and has done volunteer work in Honduras.

Foreword

When I first read the poignant story found in the introduction that is both the center and the impetus for this
book, I was filled with awe. I leaned back, speechless, until I
finally needed to get up, walk over to the window in my office,
and look out over the small lake below as I tried to absorb what
I had just read.

It was such an honestly written story of sudden loss, sadness, and surprising hope and love that I didn't know what to
think, so I finally stopped trying to make sense of it. Instead,
after a while, I sat back down, looked down at the paper that
contained it, and enjoyed being wrapped in wonder at the
spiritual journey that reflected the possibilities for all people,
particularly the young who live in this challenging world.

After a few moments of this, a thought came to me: I was
experiencing a special moment in time in Mary Beth's life that
she had captured perfectly. As a young doctoral student not
long removed from her personal epiphany, she could honestly
relay it in a way that young adults could identify with and learn
from, yet this message is profound enough to touch the wis-
est of sages. With her developing maturity and the knowledge
gained from her counseling course work and clinical practice,
she could also simultaneously reflect on it and share some of
the mysteries of faith development if she developed it further
while it was still fresh and real in her mind. The challenge was

that she would have to move quickly before this grace period passed. Fortunately for us, she did just that by journaling the experiences and understanding what would eventually provide the raw material with which to work later.

As Faith Matures: Beyond the Sunday God is not just one person's story, though. In this remarkable book she brings the experiences, questions, sorrows, joys, and practices of a number of truly remarkable people as seen through the eyes of a young person who herself is searching. Consequently, there is no glibness in the following pages, but there is hope. There is no avoidance of pain, but there is newfound meaning and maturing gleaned through the experience of suffering. Mary Beth Werdel does not offer an easy route to God, but she does respect each person's developing search for a deeper relationship with the divine...and with themselves.

Contemplative Thomas Merton once quipped that with deep faith comes deep doubt, so he suggested that we give up the business of suppressing doubt. That recognition is contained in the following pages. Mary Beth Werdel has opened the door for those who wish to deepen their relationship with the sacred. Yet she recognizes and acknowledges that how each person encounters his or her own spiritual journey is unique. Therefore, she offers no definite map because every person's destination and route is different. However, she does offer the courage, illustrations, and calling each person needs to experience in launching the next phase of life. This is truly beautiful, because what greater gift can you ask of a fellow journeyer than that?

Robert J. Wicks, Psy.D.
Author,
Riding the Dragon: 10 Lessons for Inner Strength in Challenging Times

Introduction

F or many years I worked as a campus minister at a Catholic
church for undergraduate and graduate students who attended a state university. I had an office just off campus in the
Catholic Student Center. It was a unique space—a throwback
to the 1970s in décor, inclusive of the wood paneling inside of
the building that was always noted by the students.

Yet even with vintage aesthetics, each day students found
their way to the center. Some would come for the free coffee or
the snacks that always seemed to be in the kitchen. Others came
to rest on the large oversized couch in my office in between
classes or to help with volunteer activities at soup kitchens or
homeless shelters. Still others came seeking recommendations
for work-study, summer jobs, or scholarship applications.
While on campus, I noticed that while there were unique reasons that students carried in their heads that brought them to
the Catholic Student Center, there was a common experience
that they were carrying in their hearts. Each, in his or her way,
was holding a relationship with the sacred. Some relationships
were strong and complex, others were weak and simple, and
far many more were stuck somewhere in between the two: not
yet an adult relationship with the sacred, but not certain how
to let go of childhood faith beliefs.

There was one young woman, Stephanie, whom I knew for her whole college experience. During her freshmen year she came to church on Sunday nights and was volunteering with an after-school mentoring program once a week at a local children's home. By her sophomore year, she was a committed volunteer to the home, not once missing a volunteer trip. During her junior year, she was part of an alternative spring-break trip to Honduras. While her peers were resting on beaches or returning to the comforts of their homes, Stephanie was planting trees and painting schools in the Honduran heat. By her senior year, she had become a eucharistic minister and was recruiting for and leading a volunteer trip to a children's home. After she graduated with her bachelor of arts in English, she went to graduate school and earned her master of arts in education. With dual degrees in hand, she turned down a job offer from the school district where she completed her teaching practicum to join the Jesuit Volunteer Corps (JVC), an Ignatian-Catholic domestic and international volunteer program.

Stephanie and I had many conversations in cars on the way to volunteer activities, in planes traveling to Central America, and later in coffee shops when our paths would cross, about how touched she was by the children whom she had met while volunteering. It was clear that Stephanie was able to see the face of God in these children smiling at her. She was able to see the short conversations with children as entryways calling her into deeper conversations with the sacred.

A few months passed, and Stephanie called to let me know she would be in Washington, D.C., the city where I was living at the time. In conversation over a cup of coffee I was able to see that Stephanie was still in a very deep conversation with God. As a result of her college years and her post-college experiences, her whole life had become an ongoing dialogue between herself and the sacred. There was nothing large or extraordinary about her development. It was a slow and gradual formation of faith. Stephanie is an example of a person who began her young-adult life with a childhood faith, as many of us do. Yet Stephanie's young-adult faith story ends much differently than many others I have met. It is not because the young adults I have met were not engaging their faith in some way. Rather, so many young adults seemed to be approaching their adult life with a childhood faith. This also rings true for many adults today.

As a doctoral student in pastoral counseling, I witnessed in classmates and clients fragile childhood relationships with God and the struggle that results when it is used as a coping mechanism for painful life transitions. I completed an internship at a center that specialized in issues related to bereavement. During this internship, I worked with a young woman, Ellen, whose eighty-year-old mother had developed cancer. Ellen's mother had given birth to Ellen when she was well into her forties. Because of this, Ellen had always been aware that her mother was older; though she still believed, as so many children do, that her mother would live forever. As a result of her mother's illness, Ellen was experiencing a great deal of pain, fears of abandonment, and a deep emptiness. In our work together, we created a holding space for her pain, normalized her grief reactions, and when needed, spoke of her distortion in thoughts.

In our conversations, Ellen lightly began to touch the sacred question of human suffering—an adult question with adult answers. Yet it became clear that Ellen was calling upon a childhood image of God for help. She had not yet become aware that adult questions go unanswered when they are asked to a childhood God. The healing that Ellen craved was unavailable, as encounters with an adult God were going unnoticed and untapped. God was whispering to Ellen, and she felt he did not exist because she was asking him to scream. Eventually, Ellen's mother went into remission. Ellen stopped coming to counseling, and if past behaviors are an indication of future behaviors, I imagine Ellen stopped listening for the voice of God that emerges in the adult life, often present to young adults in a special way.

***

Life is full of small epiphanies—brief awakenings to the presence of God that signify meaning and hope. Life is filled with entryways to the sacred: a conversation with a child, recovery from illness, and the gentle embrace of a close friend. But epiphanies can, and do, come in large ways, too, as I can vouch for in my own life.

Roughly fifteen years ago, I received a phone call that my youngest brother, seventeen years old at the time, had disappeared. Thomas, my brother, was participating in a group glacier expedition in Alaska. I was told that he had broken into a small group with two other young men. They had completed a strenuous eight-hour hike—one of many over the previous twenty-nine days that had taken place on a glacier. The group was tired, thirsty, and in need of setting up camp and cooking dinner. This was to be their last night on the glacier before group members were to return to their respective homes. Thomas offered to collect water while the other two young men set up tents. Thomas removed his hiking pack, picked up two tin buckets, and walked off in search of water. He was never to be seen again.

One bucket was recovered near a drainage hole in the glacier known as a crevasse. It is believed that, while attempting to fill one bucket from a small stream of water near the top of the crevasse, Thomas slipped, falling thousands of feet into the interior of the glacier. Many attempts were made to recover his body. All proved unsuccessful. Faced with a reality too far removed from what I had previously constructed as real, into the depths of the crevasse, too, fell my understanding of life. I remember traveling to Alaska, each family member coming from different parts of the U.S. at different times within a twenty-four-hour period. I left when there was still hope that Thomas would be found. My eldest brother left at a time when hope was slipping away. My mother, my father, another brother, and my sister boarded a plane to Alaska when prayers of remaining hope turned to prayers for the remains of the dead. It was upon word of this reality, in a field outside the base camp of the glacier expedition, that I literally fell to my knees. I placed my head in my hands. For the first time in my life, I felt completely empty. I see now how for the first time in my life I felt like I had an honest prayer to pray: "God, please greet Thomas in heaven."

I remember, too, traveling home from Alaska. My sister and I had been given the task of carrying Thomas' hiking pack back home. For purposes of the plane, the pack was placed in a large black bag. The pack was heavy, totaling around fifty pounds. It took the strength of both my sister and I together to move the pack across the Anchorage airport. Perhaps because of the shape of the bag, or the color, or the weight, or for the reason that the bag possessed all that was materially left of Thomas, I felt as if I was carrying my brother's body. I carried this image in my heart, returning home. I read the journal he kept while on the glacier, my one-way conversation with him from the grave. I looked through the pictures from the film that was developed, trying to piece together images of his final days. Each step I took with his bag brought the weight of his loss. As I read each page of his journal, as I flipped through each picture from his trip, I felt myself losing more and more of my belief in a comprehensible world.

With Thomas' body never recovered, my spirituality risked the same disappearance. I questioned everything around my brother's death, from the possibility of Thomas still being alive to the possibility of him never really having existed. I asked the same spectrum of questions about the reality of God: "Is God still alive?" "Did he ever really exist?" Spiritually, I see how I was broken. I was encountering God at this time in a very raw way. No more time for politely dialing some metaphorical prayer phone, the way I learned to talk to God in grammar school and was still using in my life as a young adult at that point. In the wake of Thomas' death, out of a type of necessity, I learned to encounter God each second of the day. We had conversations nearly every instant of the day on nearly every subject. Nothing was too big or too small to bring to God. While I was not aware of it at the time, I see now how it was at this point in my life that I began to truly own my spiritual identity. I took God out of the box I had previously placed him in and began to encounter him everywhere. For how else could I come to truly comprehend the incomprehensible event of my brother's death but enveloped in the embrace of God?

Without restricting encounters with God to prayer, I see how I started to encounter God in many places. I did not purposefully attempt to reconstruct my spirituality. Yet, upon reflection, I see all this was happening. The God of my childhood had died with Thomas. And I began the process of experiencing and deepening my relationship with the sacred as my young-adult self. While the death of my brother still is the most painful loss of my life, enduring the experience—moving through the experience—has allowed me to experience profound growth.

Yet we need not wait for great spiritual tragedy to experience great spiritual growth. For even the large epiphanies risk being missed if we do not learn to foster the small ones. There is perhaps no other age group in life where time is so available and assistance so abundant to developing a mature spiritual identity. In many ways, we are surrounded with people waiting to guide us as we seek to both ask and answer questions about life. What is missing is the conscious understanding that so many of us need help in forming these questions before we can ask them. Without forming life's major questions, our very lives may become the lived experiences of half-formed questions. And we risk never fully tapping into a sense of mystery outside of ourselves if we do not first tap into the sense of mystery within ourselves.

***

Half-formed questions are often too quickly answered before being even fully asked. I have found this to be true both in my own life and those of many others whom I have met. Unformed questions can result in unconsciously nurturing individuals and communities with a sense of increased doubt, uncertainty, and fear. The tendency to either walk away from God because the pain is too fresh or to answer these questions ourselves might keep us from encountering God as we emerge into adult faith. We risk losing relationships with others to the degrees that we lose relationship to pieces of ourselves. We experience only fragments of ourselves, of others, and of God.

Spirituality is a deep and meaningful way to meet life's questions; it is a deep and meaningful way to meet ourselves. Yet it may become dangerous at worst and trite at best if the questions are never really formed before they are answered.

Living a spiritual life, we dare to finish forming questions that the secular world may not necessarily encourage or support. And we come to live those answers with our very lives. Why would you volunteer at a soup kitchen on a Friday night, not make much money working for social-justice-minded volunteer programs, not sleep in on Sunday mornings? Why would you? In my own life, and through meeting the lives of others in various walks of life, I have noticed that they would just as well not, if not for the fact they *can't* "not." When you see a hungry person, you can close your eyes and they are forgotten; when you come to see, on any level, that the hungry person is connected to your sense of freedom, you no longer have your own eyes to close. Now you share them.

As a campus minister, through academic and clinical work as a doctoral student, through work as a practicing licensed professional counselor, through my travel in Central America (primarily Honduras), through my journey as a wife and as a parent, and my own erratic movement in faith in my personal journey, I have seen the same themes come up again and again in the people with whom I sit. This reflection is to bring the repeated themes closer to home. As is the case in any experiential book, this reflection is not necessarily about providing answers (as much as answers do provide immediate relief); it is about gaining perspective in order to form the questions; it is about becoming aware of how spirituality can hold the anxiety that exists in between the process of forming and the act of holding a question.

The very process of creating a space for the sacred to dwell is an invitation from ourselves for a relationship with the sacred. When we invite the sacred into a relationship, we see the encounters with the sacred are not reserved for Sunday mornings or nighttime prayers. Spirituality is deeply ingrained in our personality. The light of the sacred is palpable in every instance, every breath of life—from the very first to the very last and all that comes in between. With this understanding, we may come to live a deeper, fuller, more joyful life, in constant relationship with others and with the sacred. What more can one ask?

Chapter 1

Our Images of Ourselves, Our Images of God

I met Amy during graduate school. She was a smart, confident, charismatic woman with seemingly endless energy and enthusiasm toward life. We became friends immediately. She had what she described as the most magnificent job she could ever imagine working in public relations. In many ways her job seemed to be magnificent to me as well, for it tapped into her personal and professional strengths in a way that made her work feel more like play. She loved going to work. She loved the projects she managed, the pace of the job, and the people she came to meet along the way. She loved the life that was unfolding before her eyes.

However, the work that she loved was not to be permanent. When the American economy hit a recession, the company that she was working for dissolved. Amy, like many others, lost her job. As a result, Amy started on what would prove to be a very long search for employment and, in parallel, a very long look at her "self."

Amy and I had several conversations about the many losses that resulted from her lack of employment: the loss

1

of her financial security, the loss of her much-needed health insurance, and most concerning emotionally, the loss of her hope in what may lie ahead. As weeks turned into months and months turned into years, our conversations seemed to focus on what was starting to feel like the loss of her sense of self. I heard her repeatedly ask, over and over again, in a number of different ways, the same underlying question: "Who am I?" Amy was deeply engaged with the question of the image she had of herself. The lack of employment challenged her sense of self as a strong, confident, energetic person. And she was living the response to her question in her confusion and frustration toward life. What started as a loss of a job had fueled what psychologists would term a true identity crisis. In our conversations, with expressions of both anger and sadness, we talked about this, too.

I had met Amy at church. So I knew, on some level, she had a meaningful faith there to be a resource for her in so many different ways. I knew Amy prayed to God and that she tried to listen for his voice. I knew she had spoken before about the "will of God," though sometimes in doing so it seemed to me it was in a way that expressed a bit of magical thinking rather than a mature faith. Still, I knew Amy cared about God and held a belief that sometimes flickered into a hope that God cared about her, too.

Yet in all our conversations that centered on her image of herself, not once did Amy speak of her image of God. The ideas were two distinct constructs, divorced in Amy's mind, as seems to be the case for many people whom I have met who hold similar questions around an image of self. I started to wonder for myself why, if God is among us and within us, would we ever divorce the two images? More importantly perhaps, I started to wonder about the result of divorcing the image of self and the image of God, as seemed to be not only present in Amy's life, but also in my own.

After three years of looking for employment, Amy eventually found a job. I was happy for her in that her new job raised not only her sense of financial security but her self-esteem as well. It allowed her access to a health insurance plan so she could once again fully attend to her ongoing medical concern. It allowed her to re-enter her field with a new sense of determination and passion. But a part of me was saddened, too. Not that Amy had found employment, but rather that the job Amy found had caused her to stop engaging with the question of her image of self before she intentionally noted the deeply spiritual nature of her question. Engaging the difficult questions help us to understand the God who is with us at every moment, transforming our previous understanding of God into a more mature and less-charted faith reality.

Questioning self-identity provides an opportunity to deepen one's experience of God if one chooses to do so. However, for the question to be an entryway into a more mature experience of faith, we first must recognize the spiritual nature of the question. This requires us to begin to acknowledge the spiritual nature of ourselves. Sadly, I think this is often missed. If we do not consider our full self to include a spiritual identity, the answers to questions of self-identity and the life that one in turn leads risks being experienced as having less purpose and meaning and risks being filled with less gratitude and hope. However, if we can bring the question of God into a question of self, space is made available for the answers relative to the self to become more than would be possible when the self is imaged in isolation. I have seen in my own life what becomes possible when one considers her image of self and her image of God simultaneously.

When my brother Thomas died, I felt a great sadness that I had never encountered before. I didn't often wish to acknowledge my sadness because it didn't feel good to do so. However, even more than the discomfort of the feeling, it was difficult for me to acknowledge such sadness because on some basic level I feared being consumed by it. Still, in moments when I was able to sit honestly with myself, there the sadness was, holding inside of it many questions: What has become of Thomas? What has become of me? What is the purpose of this life? Can I ever come to feel joy again? Does this sadness have a bottom? Now that I have fallen, do I have the strength to get up? When I leaned back from my individual questions just a bit, I could see how my various concerns had roots in one larger question: "Who am I really?"

I was not entirely sure. The cognitive frame from which I imaged myself and the world had shattered before me. I sat, surrounded by the wreckage, feeling very alone. I sat for a moment believing that it was up to me, and me alone, to answer my questions of self, and so I began to feel lonelier still. So, as I do sometimes, I began to wonder if my cognitions were not refutable. I began to wonder if my thoughts that had become beliefs were not entirely true. If I am a spiritual being, does God not have something to say about my image of self? Even more, can I really begin to understand who I am without wondering at the same time about the image I hold of God? Must I not attempt to ask the question of image of self and image of God together if I ever hope to begin to answer either? Is it not I who must invite God into my questioning of self if he is ever to be present with me or if I am ever to move closer to understanding who I really am?

So, for the first time in life, I purposefully sought to image myself and God relationally. With no obvious answers, I spent a good deal of time wondering about God and about myself as I moved about my days. I wondered while walking to work; I wondered while waiting for the bus; I wondered while sitting at my computer. I wondered while grocery shopping. I wondered while eating dinner; I wondered while talking with friends and family; I wondered as I lay in my bed at night. I kept wondering and wondering. I kept the questions of self and God together alive within me. Even though my wonders did not quickly result in any type of answer to my questions, they allowed me to experience a sense of movement. It was in such motion that I started to feel less alone.

With time, I started to feel as though I was on an expedition. Just as Thomas was an explorer in Alaska, so I began to see myself as an explorer of my "self." I was journeying toward an understanding that I could not find in the familiar spaces where I had previously been, in the places and ways that felt like home. The terrain I was traveling was sometimes icy, sometimes rough, and sometimes cold. No matter which path I set out to explore, the journey always seemed to bring me to the edge of the crevasse; to the edge of the very dark abyss that seemingly physically swallowed my brother whole and threatened to do the same emotionally to me. Soon I came to realize that if I was ever to understand who I was as a person in the wake of such tragedy and profound sadness, I needed to face the great existential questions of the comprehensibility and significance of life and death. Before I could leave my Alaska, I needed to descend into the crevasse in search of signs of Thomas' death and signs of my life. And so I started to climb.

It was in this purposeful descent in search of my "self" that

I started to image God as climbing rope, something I certainly had not done before. The rope was wrapped around me, holding me safe, allowing me to keep my eyes and heart open in the darkness that scared me, allowing me to climb as long and as deep as I needed to go. In this experience of self-descent, I experienced the climbing rope paradoxically as durable enough to hold me yet light enough to not weigh me down. Sometimes the rope was so much a part of me that I forgot it was there. Sometimes I would lose secure footing, and the rope pulled me tight; sometimes the rope saved me. With such images in mind, I came to understand the paradoxes that were intrinsically part of my human existence. I became aware that I was a person who was strong enough to hold deep sadness and simultaneously able to honor the great brightness that still existed inside of me, that exists inside of us all. I was able to acknowledge my gratitude for my new perspective of life after Thomas' death without trivializing death or my grief. I could have and hold both gratitude and grief. I came to recognize and honor the ability that we have all been given to hold such paradoxes—light that emerges in darkness, joy that grows from struggle, love birthed in pain.

In my search for self in a parallel search for a deeper understanding both for and of the sacred, I felt little distance between myself and God. He was accessibly close to me in a time I needed him most. He was not merely a hope; he was not merely a cognition. He was with me; he was part of me. And I was on my way to feeling that I was part of him.

If I had not brought an image of God into the question of this image of myself, I would have created a chasm between God and me. I would have created space that is not easily traversed, not easily bridged, in what can already be a difficult relationship to truly access. If I had not brought an image of God into the conversations of my images of self, I would not only have missed an opportunity to know God better but an opportunity to know myself better. For without simultaneously seeking God, I do not believe I could have looked so long, so deeply, so honestly at the darkness within and around me. Without God I would not have had the courage to lower myself far enough into the darkness to confront the sadness I feared, nor the strength to then climb high enough out into the light to meet my so-longed-for joy. Without wondering about God, I never would have claimed pieces of myself that I now understand have always belonged to me.

Questioning my image of self and my image of God is not a one-time experience; it is a constant endeavor. As I move through life, I need to continue to hold both questions together even when I have no answers for either. Perhaps, especially when I have no answers. For if I do not continue to wonder about my image of self and my image of God together, I am restricted. I am limited. I am fettered. I may only ever come to dream of an image of who I wish to be and so would never come to consider the more that God may be calling me to be. By questioning myself as I question God, I find myself able to grow more genuinely into myself and in turn grow more genuinely into the God who imaged me first.

Chapter 2

Owning Our Spiritual Heritage

My faith life started with my mother, as did the faith life of each of my four siblings. Less like a mother duck with her doting ducklings following along in tow and more like a gaggle of wild turkeys, each Sunday, without exception, my mother on her own brought us to Mass. While at the time it was not obvious to me as to why it was necessary that I attend Mass every week, it was clear to me that my mother attended Mass for a number of different reasons. My mother went because she loved the Mass. She went because she loved her community. She went because she loved her faith. She went because, more than all else, she loved God. It was in Mass that I first heard my mother, in a loud voice, sing praises to God. And it was in Mass that I first saw my mother, in a quiet moment, cry. In Mass, unlike in other places and spaces, my mother seemed to feel as though she could be, in the presence of God, completely herself. In Mass, she was whole.

Beyond the reasons that centered on her personally, it was also clear that my mother went to Mass for other reasons. Perhaps the most obvious to me was her attendance at Mass for her children, her attendance for me. My mother went to Mass to encourage our faith development. She went to teach us about the Eucharist. She went to engage us in a faith community. She went to introduce us to God. However, I see now, from beyond my childhood faith experiences, how the God she was introducing us to, the experience of faith that she hoped to encourage, was something all at the same time deeply rooted in, and well beyond, Sunday Mass. There was more mystery to experience than merely a "Sunday God."

I have a memory of one Sunday Mass that I still find myself turning over in my head years later for what I may continue to learn from it. I was perhaps nine years old, my other siblings between thirteen and four. One Sunday, the collection basket came and Thomas, the youngest, reached into his coat pocket, secured his small, blue, hand-me-down Velcro wallet, and proceeded to, without any prompting, empty his entire four-year-old life savings into the collection basket. I remember wondering why Thomas would ever do such a thing. In a state of confusion, I looked to my mother for her response. My mother, who had indeed witnessed the event, offered no criticism or praise. She did not turn to each of us during or after Mass and use Thomas as an example of how we were to be. She didn't follow Thomas' example and empty her wallet in the same way. Rather, she smiled softly, and gave Thomas a small, one-armed embrace from her seat as she continued to sing the offertory hymn. In that moment she encouraged Thomas' faith development and so many years later, when I reflect upon it by witnessing her interaction with Thomas, in small ways she was encouraging my own.

As I grew older I was allowed to witness moments that served as testimonials to my mother's faith, revealing it to be something deep and wonderful that lived well outside of Sunday, well beyond the Sunday God of my childhood that she first introduced to me. Her faith was something different, something closer, something more complex.

One such instance happened in a family meeting with the priest at my mother's parish when we were together to prepare the memorial service for Thomas. Together we chose the readings and the hymns. Together we talked about processionals and recessionals. Together we talked about lectors and eucharistic ministers. And together we pieced together proclamations of sorrow and love. In one moment, when her tears were dry, I remember my mother sharing the phrase, "I was lucky to have known Thomas for as long as I did." I sat confused again. How can she express such a belief in this moment? Where was her anger? Where was her sadness? Where was her hurt and her rage? How could she feel gratitude in a moment of profound grief? How mature is my mother's faith? How immature is mine?

By nature, our faith has to start as immature. This is normal and natural. It makes sense that our relationship with God starts on Sunday. It makes sense that we first experience God as a Sunday God. Yet while it is the case for many, this is not where our relationship has to end. God does not need to be limited to Sunday. If we do so, we may miss the God who exists elsewhere. Indeed, our Sunday God may grow ever more difficult to locate. We may not be able to access God in moments of great pain and struggle when he is needed most deeply. We may miss opportunities to express our gratitude, to live a grateful life, and the subsequent joy that may be experienced from doing so. And we may not be able to recognize the intrinsically good things that exist in our lives even in the most difficult and trying of moments.

Yet for our faith to mature we have to take the spiritual heritage our mentors are offering to us and engage it. We have to allow it to become ours. We have to want it to become ours. We have to work to claim it as ours. We have to acknowledge that while someone passed the tradition on to us, our faith has always been our own.

I realize now, in considering the ways that my mother introduced her faith to me, that she was perhaps so successful in doing so because she always recognized that her faith could not be my faith. So then while we shared the same faith, she did not set out to guide and encourage me to become like her in faith. Rather, she guided and encouraged me to become like me in faith. She did not seek for me to reconstruct her relationship with God. Rather, she was ever prayerful that I would one day find and feel my own. She affirmed my faith development by affirming me. And she did the same for each of her children. In her embrace of Thomas after he gave over his money to the collection at Mass she was doing just this. She was encouraging him to listen to his own true heart, which she knew by her faith—if he was giving from a place of honesty—could be nothing less than the voice of a loving God. Through her embrace, my mother confirmed in Thomas then, and in me now, so many years later, that by listening and responding and becoming our true selves, we become who we were meant to be, who God meant us to be. As we slowly become our true selves, through and among others, we slowly build a faith born from a spiritual heritage but bred by our own unique selves. My relationship is all at once with the same God as my mother's, but uniquely my own. And thankfully so. For one day, when my mother is no longer physically present, my faith will not be buried with her. Rather, my faith, just as my mother's, can and will continue to live in the loving embrace of God.

Having role models to pass down tradition is important in faith development. But faith is not a passive experience. Role models, like my mother has been in my life, can teach us part of faith. They can teach us about Mass. They can teach us the Our Father, the Hail Mary, and the Glory Be. They can teach us how they call to God, how they feel his presence, how they attempt to know and do God's will. They can pray with us and they can pray for us. But they cannot give us their faith.

If we are to feel the mystery present within and outside of ourselves, we have to come to own our faith for ourselves. We have to engage it for ourselves. We may borrow another's hope when life feels overwhelming. We may borrow optimism, courage, and even strength. But we need to own our own faith if it is ever to be deeply felt, if it ever is to be understood, if we are ever to find God inside and outside of Sunday, if we are ever to come to find a space or a place where, even for a fleeting moment, we also feel whole.

Chapter 3

Called to Act

On a volunteer trip to Honduras I met a small-framed man named Louis. He worked as a farmer in a rural village community in the western part of the country. He also was one of a core of three men who assisted the volunteer groups that would come to the village. Louis had a gentle presence. He walked slowly and with intention, often humming a song underneath his breath. He frequently wore the same blue-collared dress shirt, khaki pants, and a small wooden cross around his neck. As part of the volunteer experience in Honduras, Louis invited volunteers into his small clay home that he built himself. With no running water or electricity, he explained to groups of volunteers who gathered in circles on his floor about the reality of his daily life. He spoke about farming and his family. He spoke about hunger and hope. Often he smiled. Often he mentioned the name of God. It was easily apparent to anyone who met Louis that he possessed great love for his family, deep faith in God, and an overwhelming concern for the well-being and livelihood of his community. The heart of his concerns was expressed in a single phrase: "We are very poor."

One afternoon I was walking with Louis across a plot of land that was to become a fruit tree garden. He was attempting to teach me words in Spanish, inviting me, as he did others, further into his world. We walked along and he pointed to objects (trees, a wall, a bucket). He would say the Spanish word slowly and look to me to repeat it. At one moment, Louis stopped, bending down to pick up something small that his eyes had noticed in the dirt under our feet. "Friolje rojo," he said, showing me a small red bean that he now held in the palm of his hand. He looked to me to in turn repeat his words. I tried as best I could and then smiled, looking to him for correction. He only smiled back at me. Then, rather than returning that one bean to the ground, he closed his palm, carefully placing the red bean in his pocket. And our walk and my Spanish lesson continued.

As I returned to the United States, I carried this instance in my mind. I carried Louis, his family, and his community in my heart. And I started a deeper conversation with our God about poverty, injustice—about Louis and myself.

One day in conversation with the priest from the United States who coordinated the volunteer trips to Honduras, he described the poverty that existed in Honduras as violence. Poverty, as he had come to see it, was an intense force attempting to destroy the humanity and dignity of the Honduran people. Now aware of the reality, by not responding, it felt as though poverty was attempting, too, to destroy the humanity and dignity that I possessed as well. In a moment of great sadness as I was coming to a fuller awareness of the great social injustice of it all, I cried.

There are obscene inequalities in our world. Volunteer immersion opportunities in developing countries are useful experiences to bring awareness of the inequalities to our conscience. In Honduras I dug holes and planted trees. I painted benches and school walls. I taught English formally in a classroom and informally in my interactions with people. While the work was useful, there is something more to be understood from volunteer experiences when we are present with people, such as Louis, and come to feel a sense of connection, a sense of unity, a sense of home. There is great wisdom useful to a maturing faith to be found when we allow ourselves to live in relationship with the poor.

This has been true for Anne, a very wise woman and an informal spiritual mentor in my life. Anne has lived the majority of her life engaged in a very deep conversation with God. Even still, her relationship continues to deepen and her faith continues to mature as she continues to uncover the ways she encounters God in her work with the poor and marginalized.

Anne and her husband founded and for many years coordinated what is now called the Door Ministry, a social-justice-oriented outreach program at their church aimed at providing financial services to the poor in their suburban community. Anne and her husband never intend to begin a ministry. Rather, quite organically, they happened to be at their parish office one afternoon and opened a door to find standing behind it a man who was looking for help to pay a utility bill. Anne and her husband responded and the program, now known countywide as a welcoming place for the poor, began. While the program provided people in her community with some of the basic necessities to live, Anne grew to see the ministry as nothing less than a living conversation between herself and God. Through her conversations, through her life, through being with the poor, Anne became aware that when she opened the door to assist a client, she was opening the door to "beloved sons and daughters of God." Anne's lifelong experience of being herself a "beloved daughter" became a haunting question for her as she met other "beloved sons and daughters" whose lives have been filled with pain, poverty, and injustice.

As is possible when we engage our faith, her volunteer work permeated all of her life. Meeting clients through the Door Ministry served to develop not only the way Anne lived with the poor but the way Anne lives in prayer. So overwhelmed by the injustice that she continued to witness over and over again with the different names and faces that would find their way to the "Open Door" and feeling as though words were lacking to fully describe the reality, Anne found herself seeking and finding different forms of prayer. There were not enough words to pray the traditional ways she had known previously. She found her prayers growing simpler and more silent. Just as she strove not to have compassion but to *be* compassion, not to have hope but to *be* hope, she also strove not to have prayers but to *be* prayer in the way she engaged her life with the poor. Her faith was in a constant state of development as she strove to know the God she was learning to love more.

The way that Anne has come to be with the poor and to encounter God in relationship with the poor has changed Anne's understanding of God. Surprising to Anne was the realization that the *more* she came to develop her faith, and the *more* complex and meaningful her faith grew, the *less* she felt she truly knew of God. For God has revealed himself in so many ways, Anne has come to see that his mystery is boundary-less. In response to the ever-more spacious and inclusive nature of God unfolding before her, Anne finds herself often whispering this simple prayer: "I don't know who you are, but I love you."

Though not intentional, her simple prayer to God evokes images of the way she has come to meet the poor and marginalized through the Door Ministry, too. The words she proclaims further reveal how deeply intertwined Anne's experiences are of herself, God and others. Her prayer reveals a dynamic, maturing faith possible through a lifelong relationship with God. Anne shared a meditation that she wrote reflecting on the way her faith and relationship with God has developed over the years. It reads:

Oh Breath of Life,
You have breathed me out in this,
my own small and single life.
Along with moons and galaxies and vast spaces,
beside and under mountains and forests and
near the smallest wildflowers that are
never seen or picked.
I have been a part of your life.

Now you are breathing me back into yourself.
While your universe expands at amazing speeds,
And the mountains and forests continue to be,
I diminish slowly.
I am glad to grow small again and disappear;
So grateful to have been one small breath
Of your loving self.

While she wrote the prayer with consideration to the diminishments of age, as is the case with wisdom, the prayer is not merely about growing older. The prayer also echoes themes of what can happen when we hear the will of God and, without knowing the final plan, respond. The prayer speaks to an understanding that becomes possible when we let go of ideas that we are separate from those we serve. The prayer reveals an experience of life that is offered when we come to recognize in a deep way that we are part of each other and are each in turn the breath of God for one another. We come to first know and then really experience that we are living one small part of God's story, while God becomes a larger and larger part of our own life.

However, if the call to act that so many of us feel stops with our physical presence, if it ends when we leave Honduras or when we close a physical door, if we don't continue to carry it in our heads and in our hearts, if we don't acknowledge the communion we share with the poor, if we don't come to use our breath as the loving breath of God, we will miss the wisdom palpable in our encounters with the poor. We will miss the opportunity to know God through the beloved sons and daughters who bring us closer to him. We will miss the near experience of God possible only when we allow the people we serve to become not just closer to, but part of, us.

Chapter 4

Listening to the Still, Small Voice of God

We are filled with noise. Some of the noise is outside of us. It is the sounds of cars and buses moving down streets. It is the sounds of coffee grinders, car alarms, cell phones ringing, and other people's conversations. It is the sounds of horns honking, televisions playing, and fingers texting. Some of the noise is inside of us. It is the sound of our own thoughts. It is the sound of that which we and others tell ourselves that we are trying to remember and that which we and others have told us that we can't seem to forget. It is the sound of voices telling us the clothes we are supposed to wear, the car we are supposed to drive, the places we are supposed to go, and the person we are supposed to be. With all this noise inside and outside of us, we can become quite full.

So in our fullness, how are we ever to hear the voice of God? Just as it is easy to miss ever discovering our true selves, so too it is easy to miss ever discovering God. It's easy to miss the ways he lives in our encounters with each other, in our encounters with life. But this doesn't have to be so. If we intentionally try, we can quiet ourselves and the world around us enough so that the mystery that is God can become known to us—through us and through others. When we do so, we may come to find that God has been waiting consistently patient, ever hopeful that we will move more closely toward him.

Oftentimes I write in the early mornings before anyone in my house and most people outside of it are awake. Around 4 AM or so, I make my way to my computer, turning on only a small side table lamp, and sometimes not even that. The room is quiet. I am quiet. Encountering mystery comes with ease. But as 4 AM becomes 5 AM and 5 AM becomes 6 AM and 6 AM becomes sunrise, the quietness is overcome with the noise of wakefulness. I find myself wanting to speak to the night that is slipping slowly, purposefully, into day. I want to say "Don't go!" For I have noticed that there are some things about myself, about others, about God, that are so much more brilliant, so much more elegant, so much clearer in the quiet state I can find so easily in the very early morning. Of course the day begins anyway. When night turns to day and the noise of life enters, the clarity of my sight and hearing feel as though they diminish, having to compete with the noise of the world. I have come to learn that if ever I am to find God, I must learn to find silence and stillness living in the noise.

As a counselor, I am a trained listener. I recognize that to listen, and to help others to listen, I need to cultivate quietness, inside and outside of their world. This is only possible when I can cultivate quietness within me. When I am successful, the people I work with begin, sometimes for the first time, to hear each other, hear themselves, and in a way most longed for, people sometimes come to hear the still, small voice of God.

This was true for Alex, a sixteen-year-old high school sophomore. I came to meet Alex because his mother was growing concerned for his overall well-being. Alex's grades had changed from the A's of honor roll status to D's and F's, raising the risk that that Alex would not pass his sophomore year. This was most concerning to Alex's father, who had dreams of Alex being the first in his family to graduate from high school and, perhaps, even attend college. Alex's mother shared that she was most concerned about what she observed to be a change in Alex's demeanor. She recollected fondly how Alex was a sensitive, loving child who easily expressed affection. Growing up he was quick to hug his mother and had a gentle, warm presence with his younger siblings. Now, that Alex, as she described him, had disappeared. In his place was a withdrawn and distant son who would share no more than a few words under his breath with her each day. Some days, they did not even speak. Alex's mother was in great pain, living a fear that she was losing her son and uncertain of what, if anything, she could do.

Working with the family for almost a year, it became clear that Alex was in a good deal of pain as well. He was silent and stoic in his interactions with his family. But every once in a while I would observe a flicker of the Alex that his mother described when he would make a loving comment or demonstrate affection. In such instances he presented as calm. However, most of the time his silence felt restrictive, leading me to wonder if it was not serving as a defense, as protection; yet, against what it was not clear—to me, not to his parents, and not even entirely to Alex.

While sitting with the family and watching their interactions, I started to wonder, "Does young-adult Alex, the child who was described by his mother as so deeply affectionate and loving, feel loved?" It was obvious to me that Alex's parents loved him. Alex's parents demonstrated actions that revealed they did care deeply for their son, inclusive of taking him to counseling and attending parent-teacher conferences. They each worked long hours and many weekends so that they could provide Alex with all of his necessities and most of his wants. As Alex's father shared in one session, everything that they did was for their children; everything was for Alex. The food they bought, the house they lived in, the car they drove, the work they did—all was so that they could provide a "good" life for Alex.

It was after hearing Alex's father's list of all the material things that they provided that it started to become almost painfully obvious that not once in our time together did Alex's parents turn to their son and tell him directly, softly, and sincerely, that he was loved. Their worlds, their conversations, had become full. They argued about grades. They feared out loud about his future. They shared their disappointment and frustration. They shared their fatigue. They shared their struggle with finances, their jobs, and the overwhelming stress of trying to manage a family. They shared all the noise of life that was filling all the space within and between them.

As I spent time with the family, I came to see why screaming their concerns to their son was not working. They could not scream loud enough. So then what was needed was to find some small opening, somewhere in the thick, high wall that Alex had built around himself, peer through it, and whisper to him that he had always been and always would be lovable. They needed to whisper that in that present moment he was loved. When they came to realize the need to express love, they readily and easily did so. In response, Alex used all of his strength to keep his wall together, to hold back his tears. But he couldn't. The words were too powerful. They were too direct. They were too sincere. They were too desired to be heard. With the awareness of love, Alex and his parents started a journey toward finding space to speak not only about but to each other's hearts in a way where they could each be silent enough to hear.

Witnessing the interaction between Alex and his parents, I began to wonder. If we can't whisper to each other the phrases that our hearts yearn to hear, how can we expect that we will ever come to find God in our words? And if we can do this, how can we ever miss him?

As a counselor, I also worked with one brave teenager, Jeremy, who had witnessed the death of his grandfather when he was a small child. He was so young that no one in his family thought that such an experience would have an effect on him. But of course, regardless of age, such experiences can and do affect us. As an adolescent, he started to think somewhat obsessively about his grandfather's death and where, if anywhere, he was now. Jeremy was Catholic. He shared that he went to church regularly. He prayed to God. He believed in heaven. However, he was not sure if his grandfather was in heaven. He desired answers that he felt were beyond him. He desired a conversation that felt impossible. Together, we created a quiet place, away from all the noise outside of his world so that he could hear himself. In this space, Jeremy began to recollect the experience of watching his grandfather die. He began to recollect the many pieces of his relationship with his grandfather that he cherished and missed. Most importantly, he came to find the ways in which his grandfather is still alive in his life and the ways in which their relationship can and does live on. In a quiet space, Jeremy came to feel that his grandfather still loved him and that he still very much loved his grandfather. This always was and always would be true.

While I imagine God may scream at times, in my work, in the moments of connection where something sacred appears present, in the times when I have observed a person hear and feel expressions of love, I have witnessed the silence of God. I have come to realize that I am off track if I expect God to scream louder than the noise that exists in this world, if I feel I have to scream louder than the world. I am on track when I seek to quiet my world so that I may hear the voice of God and recognize it as just that.

What God may say to me in the silence I create is as unique as I am. Yet underlying all the expressions, all the encounters, all the experiences of God, in stillness and in silence, I believe God whispers expressions of love. Sometimes God whispers to us in our own thoughts, as was the case for Jeremy. Sometimes, as was true for Alex, we hear the whisper through those we love. Regardless of how, if we can come to hear these words, even once, we hold the possibility of being changed forever.

We need to find quietness to find our own early-morning experience, that place in our life where we feel closer to mystery than not. It can be difficult to do but worth the effort of trying. For once we learn how to do so, we find our desired task becomes not one of "how do I cultivate a quiet mind so that I may turn toward God," but "what more can I do to keep from ever turning away from the voice of God who I hear whispering to me, 'You are deeply loved.'"

Chapter 5

Be Still and Know I Am God

It is so difficult to be still. For almost every minute of every day, most people are moving. Of course movement can be a blessing. Sometimes we are called to move. It is our ability to move that allows us to rock restless infants, feed hungry children, and visit elderly adults. Walking, running, jumping, playing, working all can be experiences where we may encounter the sacred. Paradoxically, however, the very same acts where we may come to find God may also be acts that keep us from encountering God. The difference may lie in our intentions. Movement without intention far too easily can become chaotic. So then in order to be in motion and not to be filled with chaos, we need to balance our motion with moments of stillness, too. Purposefully carving out space for moments of stillness in our lives allows us to be in motion with more purpose, more peace, more clarity, more gratitude, and so most wonderfully, more joy.

Stillness is a conscious practice. Though we may stumble upon it by accident, it requires attention if it is to be nurtured. This became especially obvious to me in my own life one semester during my graduate studies. Finding balance can be challenging while in school. However, there was one semester that was exceptionally full. Along with taking a full course load, preparing for qualifying exams, working as a graduate assistant, working part time at a research institute, and completing my counseling internship, I was also planning my wedding. On weekdays, I would often leave my apartment at 6 AM and not stop moving until I returned home at 9 PM. My various work and school experiences had me traveling between three states. Sometimes I moved by car, sometimes by train, other times by my own legs. Regardless of how I moved, my thoughts seemed to race along just the same.

One spring day, toward the end of two semesters of chaotic movement, my motion caught up with me. I woke up when it was still dark outside and made my way around my apartment speedily getting ready for work. I showered, grabbed something to eat, quickly slipped on my shoes in the dimly lit foyer, and ran to catch the 6 AM train to work. While on the train I casually glanced down. It was only then that I noticed that I was in fact wearing two different shoes. Both were ballerina-style flats, but one was a light-brown suede with a small decorative flower atop, and the other was a patent-leather black shoe with a small bow. In embarrassment, I drew my feet underneath the train seat. I knew I did not have the time to return home. When I arrived at work, I desperately called a friend who lived nearby and wore relatively the same size shoe to beg her to bring me a pair of matching shoes. And more importantly perhaps, sitting at work awaiting my friend, I made a mental note of how all of my motion was becoming chaotic. I was losing myself. And while it was not in my mind at the time, I am aware now that opting for this way of being was losing my ability to find God.

A few weeks after, I was sitting in my apartment in Washington, D.C., working on a paper for school. My apartment was in perhaps the nosiest part of the city. Fire trucks and police cars often blasted sirens past my window. People were consistently outside shopping, eating, walking, running, biking, talking, yelling, and sometimes even screaming. I was at my desk in the back of the apartment, which offered a bit more quietness, as it faced a very small enclosed courtyard. There was just enough room for a small bench and a few trees.

Then it happened. In between a moment of typing, quite by accident, I found myself in stillness. That moment was quite memorable for it felt so foreign, so quiet, so good. Rather than returning to typing, I pulled my chair for a moment away from my desk. I took an intentional deep breath in and breathed it slowly, purposefully, out. I had found myself.

After a few moments of sitting in stillness with my breath, I heard birds chirping outside of the window for the first time ever in the four years that I lived in D.C. I was not naïve enough to believe even for a second that the birds were new. Of course they had always been there, outside of my window, singing, playing, proclaiming a bit of joy whether I was aware of them of not. They did not miss me; it was I who missed them. Most sincerely, in this moment, I began to wonder what else I may be missing besides the songs of birds in my life.

Sometimes my relationship with God is like my relationships with the D.C. birds. He is there to be in relationship with whether I am aware of him or not. In stillness, too, I realized that so much of my day is filled with talking about God, thinking about God, wondering about God. But only in stillness do I become aware of how close or far I am from him.

After this experience, well aware that I desired a mature

relationship with the sacred, I started to intentionally seek and bring moments of stillness into my life. Sometimes in the morning. Sometimes in the evening. Rarely, but usually most revealing to me, sometimes I can find moments of stillness amidst the busy day. My moments of stillness reveal to me where I am and remind me where I want to be in relationship with God. I can be almost anywhere. I may be in my bedroom, or on the train, or in a classroom before a student enters, or a counseling room before a client or family enters. I take a moment to be still and to feel in my heart what I spend so much energy hoping for with my head…that I know God and God truly knows me.

There is a piece of the Mass, after Communion, where being still comes easy. On my knees, eyes closed, head bowed, hands together. I am with God. In this moment I come repeatedly to recognize what he already knows—that I often place distance between us. In this moment I pray what he is already answering, that the space becomes thinner. I pray that as close as God feels in such a moment, that I may be drawn ever closer still. Learning to hold this dissonance between what I want my relationship to be without running from it, without being consumed by it, by uniting these two pieces of myself, through this very tension the sacred emerges.

I think we fight stillness. I am not sure why. Perhaps because it is so difficult. Perhaps because it feels unfamiliar. Perhaps because, while we deeply desire a relationship with God, so too are we deeply scared of what it may mean to have one, of how we will change and how our lives will be changed. Perhaps because in quiet meditation we may realize that on this earth, in this life, while moments of joy, moments of home, moments of peace, and encounters with God are so abundantly possible to find, they are so impossible to hold for as long as our heart truly desires.

Chapter 6

The Way to Wisdom

Considering pain as something we would open ourselves up to really feels masochistic...but it isn't. For so many years, in so many ways, the people who raised us attempted to protect us from pain. In many ways, parental figures consider this to be a piece of their role akin to feeding us. The very identity of our parents can be tied into protection from pain—feeling that they have succeeded or failed based upon the ability and degree to which they shelter their children from the experience. Of course, feeling safe and protected are key components for healthy development, and our parental figures are right in seeking this. And of course, purposefully inflicting or seeking out pain is not good by any means. However, as we grow older we all come to realize that, try as we may, pain is not entirely escapable.

With this understanding, what is of consequence then is not how we avoid painful experiences (the death of a friend or relative, the loss of a job, the end of a friendship), but rather how we meet suffering when it presents itself in our life. For as strong our reaction against staying open to pain is, avoiding or numbing our pain distances us from meeting wisdom. Far too often we hide our pain—this characteristically human experience.

Perhaps we do this because of fear; perhaps because of learned behavior. Regardless of the reason, hiding pieces of ourselves comes at the same great cost. For it is in the meeting of the deeply human places of people where relationships become transformational; while the hiding of such places can stagnate our spirituality. I was reminded of this through an encounter with my friend Lizzie.

I have known Lizzie for many years. We started going to church together in graduate school and continued to attend together regularly on Sunday mornings for years after we graduated. Quite often, she arrived early to church, and so she would wait for me by the front steps. In all the years that I met Lizzie, never once did she meet me inside of the church. It is as if she was waiting for the whole experience, the whole prayer, to be communal. I have often wondered if I did not make it one Sunday how long she would wait by that first step. And while I know it is not true, Lizzie is the type of friend who leads me emotionally to believe that she would have waited forever.

Regardless of the day, Lizzie always seemed to greet me with a smile that took over her entire face. When I sit with Lizzie, it is as if there is no one in the world she would rather be with. She has a wonderful ability to remember the small things that have big meanings—birth dates, upsets in daily schedules, and names of close friends.

Lizzie has great energy and passion as well. In social situations, she pulls everyone into the conversation by finding ways to acknowledge and encourage different perspectives. She has a gift for fostering an intellectual community in eccentrically different people. Through Lizzie, I have met the most interesting people.

In work and school, Lizzie is phenomenal. For four years, she worked full time as a paralegal during the day and went to law school part time at night and on weekends. When she graduated from law school, she quickly passed a difficult state bar on her first attempt, two major milestones in her life that she acknowledged with great humility.

Around the same time of this great joy, Lizzie's mother was diagnosed with multiple sclerosis. Lizzie almost never talked about it. On one unusual morning, over a cup of coffee after Mass, she started to share a bit. She told me that her mother was experiencing significant fatigue, muscle pain, and difficulty with balance. She shared that her mother, a once-avid cyclist who had passed her love of the sport on to her daughter, had stopped biking. In fact, she had sold her bicycle because it was too difficult for her to see it sit unused in her garage. Lizzie shared that each time she passed her own bike, hanging on a wall in her foyer, she thought of her mother and of how much she hated the letters MS.

As she shared, Lizzie's eyes slowly started to fill with tears, a normal reaction to such an overwhelmingly painful experience. Yet, after a few moments, she took a few deep breaths in, and she stopped crying. It seemed that Lizzie used all her energy, all her passion, all her strength that I had for so long admired to stop her tears. She even apologized for crying. "I'm sorry," she said. My accepting response of her tears was not enough. For rather than using her strength to open herself up to her pain, Lizzie used it to continue to close herself off.

In times of pain such as Lizzie's, when we stop our tears we stop as well such things as insight, growth, connection, and peace. While it may be thought a natural phenomenon that we only want to share the pieces of ourselves that are shining, to be whole, we must acknowledge that pain is part of the story of us. We must find ways to meet it so that we may foster it for use in our development.

We have needs as humans not to be constantly filled with sources of light but rather to develop the ability to be fully present in darkness. We cannot, and should not, ask for dark places in our life. But by living, naturally dark places occur, as they did for Lizzie, as they have for all of us. These dark, painful places can also be entryways into developing sacred sight. Once the dark places have passed, so also has our opportunity to develop this sacred skill. Some pieces of ourselves can only be understood, some aspects of our relationships can only be deepened when we stand awake in the dark.

I walked home that morning wondering why it was that such deeply human pieces of Lizzie were kept on her inside. Why do we share the pieces of ourselves that are common to all animals and hide the pieces that make our species so uniquely us and so deeply connected? Why is it in times of pain that we so readily choose isolation over intimacy?

I wondered also what inside of me might have contributed to Lizzie's desire to hide her pain. I wondered if there was something that perhaps I was doing that did not encourage her sharing. I wondered how well I really believed that it was not only all right for her to share her pain, but it was good for her to share her pain—it is good for her, for me, and for us. I wondered how I had come to form Lizzie's identity as someone who was somehow protected from the universal experience of pain. What shadow had I made of Lizzie? And what shadow had I made of our friendship?

Staying open to pain starts by the act of noticing that in life transitions we have a front-row seat to our interior world. In these moments we can truly look at ourselves. We can start to bring awareness to what it is that we are willing to share and what it is that we attempt to hide; the places where we feel forced to take a deep breath in, and the places we feel free to take a deep breath out.

If pain is a characteristically human experience, then rejecting pain is tantamount to rejecting our humanness. Rejecting our pain can lead to a rejection of growth that is possible from Lizzie's pain both for her and for me. Being in relationship with Lizzie, I also can be limited or encouraged in my own understanding and growth by Lizzie's level of openness to pain, and she can be limited or encouraged by mine. This adds a new, often unacknowledged, loss that can happen when we close ourselves off from pain; for I need Lizzie's full story to create meaning and understanding in my own life. Likewise, she needs the whole of mine to create meaning and understanding in her life. When I close my life from pain, Lizzie suffers. When I open myself up to pain, Lizzie's pain does not dissipate, but her loneliness does; her separateness does; her suffering does.

I never asked Lizzie why she was closing up. I was not yet aware that in my interactions with Lizzie I was unconsciously living an answer to the question, "How can I encourage my friend to do something that I have not yet fully mastered?" With my question now conscious, I am free to form an answer that comes from the understanding that we are, at our cores, processes not products. This is why we need to have constant prayer. Yesterday's prayer is not enough for today. Tomorrow's prayer for yesterday can only be of forgiveness.

I pray for Lizzie many Sunday nights, for often our encounters are fresh in my heart. I pray that along with seeing her power, her passion, and her energy, that I may come to know her grief, her pain; that I may come to know all of her. I pray that I may notice the places within myself that I have closed off from tears. I pray for the strength to open such places, both for the benefit of me and for those with whom I am in relationship. I pray that I may not quickly fill such places, but leave them open so that they may be filled with wisdom for encountering the sacred.

Chapter 7

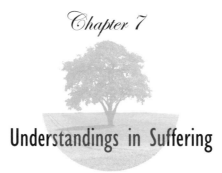

Understandings in Suffering

I t was Friday morning. My husband and I had both blocked the day from work. Our lives had started to feel very full, so we decided to carve out time to be with each other and our two children. We talked about maybe going out to breakfast; maybe we would go to a children's bookstore; definitely we would spend some time at the playground. Beyond that nothing was planned.

Our computer sat on the desk in our bedroom. It was opened to a web page that contained my e-mail. My husband walked past it and casually noticed the first lines of an e-mail that had been sent to me. He brought my attention to it. The words read, "Some very sad news…." As I started to read the little bit of information contained in the e-mail, my hands went quickly and forcefully to my chest. It was an attempt perhaps to ground myself in my heart, to know that it was still beating, to know that this was not some horrific dream. The e-mail explained how a dear friend of mine had been shot, one of two recipients of a somewhat random and very violent act performed by an angry, unstable man with a gun. It seemed that after shooting my friend he later killed himself. While the other victim died immediately, my friend was, at the time of the e-mail, in critical condition. She had been brought to a shock and trauma center, where she had been placed on life support. She was not expected to make it through the night.

I sat at my desk in utter disbelief and quietly proclaimed: "No. No. No." How could this be?

I met her during my doctoral work. We were both students. I looked up to her for many years. And then, slowly, thankfully, we became friends. Though even as friends, I still looked up to her in many ways. Not necessarily for what she did (though this was remarkable too), but more so for the way she lived her life and for the encouragement that she provided me in living mine.

My friend seemed to be able to do it all. She was the rector at an Episcopal parish. She was an affiliate faculty member of pastoral care and a counseling graduate program. She was a counselor and researcher with specializations in working with those in trauma. She ministered to the dying and the bereaved. And she did it all in a beautiful, energetic, sincere way. While her days were certainly full, she was consistently kind, caring, and loving toward me. This is not an easy way to live. It is easy to become angry or bitter or resentful when our days are full. It is easy to block people out—in little ways (by not being fully present with them in conversations) or in big ways (by simply ignoring them completely). Thankfully this was not how she lived her life; this was not how I experienced our friendship.

My friend always found a way to remain available. My friend always promptly picked up the phone or returned a voice mail message or an e-mail. She always made time to talk, even when she really didn't have time. She would help me process anything in my life that I was having problems with no matter how big or small. So when I heard the news that she had been shot, I looked for my phone and thought of whom I could call to talk about such a tragic event. While there were many people who would willingly listen, I only wanted to call her. Without her there to process the event, I started to do it alone. I started to think about the blessing that she was in my life and began to recollect the last time we had spoken, just two weeks earlier to wish each other a blessed Easter. I started to wonder if I would ever have the opportunity to speak with her again. I started to wonder about the moments before she was shot. Was she scared? Could she see what was happening? Did she scream? What were her last words? It was familiar territory. To wonder about the last moments of a loved one's life that I knew had no answers. I became overwhelmed by a number of feelings. I thought to myself: Not her. Not now. Not again. Didn't I already learn this lesson? Didn't I already move through this? But of course while previous loss can be an opportunity to grow in faith, moving through it successfully does not keep us from meeting it again. Loss is a lesson that we are asked to meet many more times than once.

I had to travel to Baltimore for her funeral. It was about four hours away. With two children both under two years old, getting to the funeral was a bit more complex than traveling the four hours. My sister came to help. I was aware that I was having a difficult time staying present in the moments before I left. I was moving in a hurried way around my apartment gathering my things and explaining the routine to my sister. In the midst of talking to my sister about bottles and meals and nap times and emergency numbers, I was trying to also prepare my 23-month-old for my departure. He could tell I was getting ready to go somewhere. My anxiety was transferring to him.

While I recognize that my son did not need to have all the information of my journey, I recognized too that there was some information that he needed to have to help him feel at ease. So I told my son I was going to a place called Baltimore. I told him I was taking the train. I told him I would not be home for dinner but that his dad and his aunt would be with him. I told him I would be home later that night after he was already sleeping. I promised him I would check on him when I returned, that I would be certain to make sure he was tucked in well and to see that all of his stuffed animal friends were just where he liked them. He then asked me with his two-year-old vocabulary why I was going to Baltimore. So I told him, "Mommy is going to Baltimore to say good-bye to a friend." I then I gave him a hug, told him I loved him very much and while my intention was to say good-bye to my friend, I left wondering if I would be able to do so.

Sitting at the funeral was one of the first moments I had to myself that I did not need to multi-task grieving with child-care. The full reality of my friend's death came to me. My eyes quickly filled with tears. I was fighting the suffering intrinsic in her death; I was fighting my good-bye. Instead of being in my heart, I found myself turning to my head. I was turning over an idea that my husband had shared with me about her death. In one of the many conversations we had about the death of my friend, he shared that he believed that the tragedy was not only that she died but she had been robbed of her death. By that he meant that because of the manner in which she died, because it happened in an instance before her body was worn by time or age or disease, she did not get the opportunity to experience the process of dying. There was no process; there was no experience for her or for those who loved her. There was no time to experience a reciprocal good-bye. And while the suffering would still exist in the loss regardless, the pain perhaps would be different.

And so I began to think about how my friend would have been if she had been given the opportunity to have a death. Quite easily it came to me that I held a belief that she would have experienced the process of dying well. I imagined that she would have been strong and compassionate and understanding and humorous and sweet. She would have been encouraging and honest and available. I imagined she would have been this way in death because I knew her to be that way in life. For how can we not be in death anyone but who we are in life? Aren't we all in the process of dying each moment? Does holding an understanding such as this have the ability to change the way we live?

Then I started to wonder about me, my own life, and my own death. I wondered how I would be in death? I wondered how I was living in that moment of life. How similar or different was I from the way my friend valiantly lived her life? There were many words that came to my mind in response to my questions. Yet all the different ideas and feelings led me to one core understanding; I was further away from dying well than I wanted to be. After the funeral, on my train ride home, I let the questions of how I wanted to live and die breathe inside all of me, not just in my head. Most importantly, I let them into my heart. In doing so, I started to feel closer to God. In doing so, I became aware of many things.

I realized that while I want to live life seeking God, my goal is not perfection. For when perfection is on my horizon, I too easily become paralyzed by guilt; I too readily become narrow in my thinking. So, too, I realized while I want a life of conviction in my faith, my goal is not to be oppositional in doing so. For when I focus too much on being right, I isolate myself from the people I believe are wrong, and so I isolate myself from the learning that is possible through being in relationship with them. I cut myself off, rather than open myself up. And a part of living and dying well demands a sense of openness.

Being part of my friend's life, sitting in her funeral, reflecting on her death and my own, in the process of finding the way a way to say good-bye, I realized that what I really want is to live life delicately interacting with the world and others genuinely and compassionately. What I really want is to live moments of life with sincerity and not reluctance. What I really want is to live life in the most honest, caring, loving way possible that I can in any given moment. What I really want is to live life full of spirit and full of the Spirit, just as I had witnessed in the life of my friend. What I really want is a rich, meaningful life. What I really want is to be a person who lives this life with an elegant spirituality; and what I really want is to be a person who dies with the same. And if ever I am to have even a chance of living such a life and so having such a death, I need to constantly seek my God. And I need to find strength in a community of people who sometimes peacefully, sometimes desperately, but always prayerfully seek him, too.

When I returned home, my oldest son was in fact still awake. So I sat with him in the rocking chair in his room. He shared with me, in his two-year-old vocabulary, the events of his day and we rocked and rocked and rocked and rocked until he finally fell asleep. We rocked until I realized that on my trip to Baltimore I did indeed start to say good-bye to my friend. We rocked until I realized that even though my friend had not had a death process, she was, past her death, encouraging mine. We rocked until I came to realize how magnificent it was that I had been blessed with the complexity of being that allowed me to hold together a sleeping child peacefully in my arms, a good-bye to my friend sadly in my heart, and the idea of living an elegant spiritual life freshly in my mind. We rocked until I realized that I was, in this moment in time so sacredly holding them all. We rocked until I realized my prayer that I may come to find some way of being that would allow me to hold my child, my friend, and a rich and meaningful life not only in that moment, but forever. We rocked until I realized that this hope is most alive and most possible in grounded relationship with the sacred.

Chapter 8

Seeing Oneself Kindly

We are all born into love. God loves us long before the moment we take our first screaming breath and well past the moment we take our last. Sadly, and for many reasons, this love is not always accessible from the people we need it most deeply from...our parents. When this happens, how we come to see ourselves can become quite negative. We may learn a self-talk that comes to image ourselves repeatedly throughout the day, and throughout our actions as stupid, worthless, pathetic, and unlovable. Sadly, this was true for a friend of mine named James.

James had a very difficult childhood. He was the victim of paternal emotional and physical abuse for sixteen years until his mother worked up enough courage to leave his father. James' father was not always abusive. There were times when he showed a kind interest in James' mother and James' two younger siblings. However, James never felt that such kindness was ever extended toward him. The best he could hope for, he explained, was to be ignored. The moments of kind interest that James' father portrayed were perhaps worse for his young developing image of self than if his father had demonstrated none. For what James came to learn in such moments when his father showed mercy was that there was something fundamentally wrong, not with his father, but with himself. Others in his family managed to win his father's affection at times, but James, no matter how hard he tried, simply could not. "There must," James thought, "be something fundamentally wrong with me."

Like so many people I have come to know who have been victims of childhood abuse and have not had access to counseling or therapeutic relationships after the abuse, James developed a profoundly negative view of himself. Understandably so, this negative self-image was very much part of his young-adult self.

Once James and I made plans to spend the day hiking in the mountains two hours north of my house. We planned to meet at my house at 6 AM so we could finish our hike before the heat of the July sun set in. On the morning we were scheduled to meet, James had awakened late by accident. He arrived at my house at 6:45 AM. He apologized excessively and called himself stupid multiple times in my presence. I repeatedly assured him that his lateness was not a problem. I even suggested a shorter trail we could hike so we could still be back in the air-conditioned car before the heat grew too unbearable. However, throughout the drive north, James continued to apologize. James did not believe my words. In his eyes, his tardiness was simply one more example of his terribleness. James' negative self-talk had become so ingrained that he could see no other fault in situations such as this other than with himself.

Since I was not in a therapeutic role with James, I was careful not to take on the role of counselor. However, being his friend, being a person who cared about him and his well-being,

I asked him if he was aware of how poorly he spoke of himself. I asked him if he ever thought that perhaps that negative voice he had adopted was not his true voice, not the voice that he was born to have and proclaim. Perhaps unsurprisingly, James could see no other self-image and could blame no other person than himself.

Later that morning, as we hiked together, I found myself in a quiet, prayerful moment feeling very saddened: saddened by the idea that a person could not imagine any view of himself other than negative; saddened by the great darkness in James' inner world; saddened by the idea that my words seemed to offer him no help in finding or feeling light; saddened that James' negative image was serving in some ways to fulfill a belief that he was unlovable.

While James never spoke of God other than to say that he only went to church when he went home to visit his mother, and he only went for his mother's sake, I imagined James' view of God was negative as well. I imagined at some point in his life he may have questioned (or perhaps more likely answered the question without consciously asking it) how the loving God that his mother believed in so deeply would allow his father, her ex-husband, to have hurt him so deeply. I imagined I would, too, had I had the early-childhood experiences of James.

Our early relationships are so important in forming how we come to see ourselves. Our early relationships help us to image the likeness of God. James' father nurtured not a child filled with faith and hope, but one filled with fear and insecurity. James had come to believe, like his father, that he was worthless. He could do no right. It did not matter how hard he tried, how deeply he desired his father's affection and protection, because when James did things right, his father still rejected him.

In spending time with James, I recognized that I could not heal him in the role of friendship alone. James needed more guidance and structure than I alone could manifest. But I was not hopeless. I was not paralyzed. While I did not cause his negative self-view and I could not take it away, I could still be of use. I could serve as an example in my interactions and help him believe that he is not all bad, that he can and often does do right. I could assure him that he is good, that he does have worth and that he is lovable. I believed this. And in my heart I know God believes this, too.

Of course, abuse victims are not the only ones who risk having negative views of themselves. We all have the ability to treat ourselves unkindly. Words, ideas, fears, and self-doubts exist. We have a spiritual shadow, the part of us that is in darkness, caused because something gets in the way of the source of light. And while the voices may have many origins (perhaps our father or mother, a childhood bully, an adult coworker, a supposed friend), in the end, no matter whose voice first proclaimed cruel words, we must remember that it is our voice, our thoughts, our beliefs that keeps them alive. We get in our own way of seeing ourselves kindly.

It is not an inflated sense of self that is necessary. James doesn't need to believe that he does everything perfectly well, that he is incapable of making a mistake, that he has no growing edges. This is just as illusionary and dangerous as the idea that he is worthless. This is just as destructive. And it blinds us just as much from coming to see the face of God.

I remind myself in moments when I am less than perfect to see myself with kind eyes. Sometimes I am even fortunate enough to have others around to help me to remember. When I find myself with negative self-images, I try to simply interrupt my negative thoughts and be gentle with myself. I do it not only for me but for all the people with whom I am in relationship, too. For do I not need to see myself kindly so that I may see others I love—such as James—kindly, too?

When we miss this gentleness, or, even worse, lose or challenge this gentleness, we lose or challenge the full, loving sense of the person before us. We lose or challenge the full, loving sense of the God who visions us into life. So then seeing ourselves kindly is not something simply nice to do. Seeing ourselves kindly is a deeply spiritual act that takes great patience and practice. When we begin to incorporate this spiritual act into our way of being in this world, we may come to see ourselves and others with the eyes of God.

Chapter 9

Our Spiritual Teachers

We all have spiritual gifts. We all have aspects of ourselves that quite simply shine. Perhaps we are blessed with a mind for organization; perhaps we move easily to a place of deep reflection; or maybe we most readily make space for other people in our lives. Our gifts are indeed from a loving God. When they are nurtured they allow us to easily encounter ourselves, each other, and God in deep and meaningful ways. They help us to experience meaning, purpose, passion, and joy. Awareness of our spiritual gifts can move us to understand a deeper meaning of the experiences of gratitude and grace.

However, through reflection, we can come to see how the extreme of our spiritual gifts can cast a spiritual shadow and become our spiritual limitation, our growing edge. While we may at first have a desire to run from or ignore our spiritual shadows, we should try not to. For I have seen in my own life and in the lives of people I have met how our shadows can be great spiritual teachers in the context our lives. Through intentionally reflecting on the experiences in life that annoy, anger, or simply bother us, we can come to know our shadows better. The insight that can be acquired through reflection can then in turn become a first step in softening our growing edges and so deepening our spirituality.

Take for instance a young woman I know named Kate. She was a committed person. In relationships, in work, even in her "play" she possessed great loyalty and an enormously strong drive to be fully present in the task or relationship at hand, and in doing so to work toward success. It was her commitment to her relationships that allowed her to remain friends with a number of people in her life even though they had moved geographically very far away. And it was her commitment to school and work that allowed her to succeed in academics that eventually led her to acceptance into one of the top law schools in the country. Commitment came easily to her. It was a gift. In fact, she found it difficult to live any other way than engaged in the world in a committed way. Doing so often produced feelings of joy.

However, in extreme cases, the same commitment that allowed her to experience life in a meaningful way was the source of great pain. Extreme commitment can be an indicator that a person has difficulties letting go. Kate found it very challenging to let go when life presented the necessity to do so. In relationships, when the attention of the other started to drift, she had a tendency to respond with a desire to hold people even more closely. The result, of course, is that she ended up pushing people even further away. In work, she found it difficult to accept any court decision that was not in her favor. She would refuse to allow herself to integrate the information into her cognition. She would obsessively continue to argue for her stance. She would have trouble eating, sleeping, and relaxing in the days and weeks after a case was lost. It became clear that in extreme cases, her commitment served to close her off from experiencing life rather than to open her up. And for us to find and nurture meaningful relationships with the sacred, we need one particular attribute more than others, namely to be open.

Kate did not need to give up her commitment; to do so would be tantamount to not accepting her gift. However, if Kate wants to fully access her gift, she must balance it with a healthy ability to learn to let go. Maturing our relationship with God becomes possible when we start to nurture our gifts. To do thus, we do not need to grow wider, but rather we are called to grow deeper.

The necessary softening of our spiritual limitations can only happen, though, when we take time to look at ourselves. While this can be a difficult task, it can be even more difficult when our spiritual limitations become evident in our relationships with others, as they so often do.

This was the case for two of my friends, Jen and Heather, who found themselves part of a very long fight. It was one of those arguments that gets away from itself. They had not spoken to each other for almost two years. This longstanding argument clouded reality; with so much time passed, the actual facts of the argument are muddy. Even without the construct of time, arguments tend to cloud our judgment. For we each hold a perspective as truth; and we mistake small "t" truth with large "T" Truth. When this happens, reconciliation can become difficult at best. And so while extreme, also somewhat predictably, Jen had convinced herself that she held the only truth that could possibly be known and decided that Heather was wrong in her understanding of truth. Therefore, she made up her mind that she would write Heather out of her life.

Heather reached out to Jen, asking that they agree to disagree and move forward with their relationship, perhaps not as friends but as peers. She sought to put the fight behind them and was open, honest, and loving in her approach. Sadly, Jen did not respond. Still, Heather possessed a gift of sensitivity that allowed her to be both understanding and determined in her pursuit for a resolution. She reached out a second time, but again, Jen did not respond.

Over the two years, oftentimes in my conversations with Jen, the topic of Heather would come up. And oftentimes in my conversations with Heather, the topic of Jen would come up. Perhaps because they knew I maintained a relationship with both. Perhaps, I hoped, because they both still held a desire for resolution.

However, in a recent conversation Heather declared to me that she was no longer interested in a relationship with Jen. My heart sank. It seemed that while Heather's gift of sensitivity was that which at first allowed her to extend outward toward Jen, it was an extreme case of sensitivity that now drew her inward. She was hurt, and this hurt quickly turned to anger. She could no longer see Jen. Her sensitivity blinded her. While at first it was her sensitivity that allowed her to see the woundedness that both she and Jen shared, this sight was no longer available. Heather was only able to see her own wounds.

As I listened to Heather, I started to understand that her experience with Jen was presenting her with an opportunity to learn about the extreme of her spiritual gift. And I wondered if she would take it. I then started to wonder why it is that we write off the very people that have the most to teach us. In the case of Jen and Heather, Jen could teach Heather something about her spirituality that I, a cherished friend, could not.

At one point in our conversation, Heather asked me a number of questions: "Why should she continue to be available to a person who did not desire a relationship with her?" "Why would she put herself in such a discomforting position?" "Why would she choose to not feel good?" So I wondered why with her. What would make someone leave a place in her heart open for a person who did not desire a relationship? I wasn't entirely sure at first. And then in a moment of clarity it came to me. We do so because that is the definition of compassion. We do so because that is what we are called to do. We do so because that is who we are called to be. We do so because God does so for us. We reject God in so many different ways so often during the day. And yet the door is always left open. We always get another chance.

Compassion means that we continue to care about another person's pain. We continue to hope that her suffering will end. It is not about pouring salt on an open wound. Heather's gift of sensitivity allowed her to see this. However, Heather's spiritual limitation was not allowing her to see that we need to leave our wounds clean and open—let them have air. For this is the only way that they may truly heal.

When things go awry, we seek God. We want him to comfort us. We want him to remember us. We want him to be available and loving and forgiving. We want him to be compassionate. And I believe that he asks the same of us in return. He wants us to be open, to remember him, to be available, to be loving, forgiving, and compassionate people. He desires that we keep our minds and our hearts turned toward him. Compassion can come easily if we understand the need we have to remember. We need to remember our suffering when we feel joy. We need to remember our weaknesses when we feel strong. We need to remember out hurts when we feel comfort. And we need to respond in a way that does not match the other person in a relationship. We need to respond in a way that seeks to mimic God's response. Of course we do not want to put ourselves in harm's way. Of course we need to understand physical and emotional abuse and place limits on pieces of relationships that are safety concerns, physical and emotional. But we need not place limits on our spirituality. Even if we can never see a person again because of real safety issues, we can always pray—pray for his conversion. Pray for his change of heart and mind. Pray that we may learn and grow.

Each relationship we have holds something to teach us about the sacred. There is always something for us to learn. I have come to understand that if there is any hope for understanding the spiritual answers in life experiences, we have to look for and ask the spiritual questions. I don't know the entirety of all that Heather can learn by staying open to Jen. It is her journey, her learning. Yet I pray that she will, as I pray, too, that I will have the courage and strength to remain open in the times ahead of me when unconventional spiritual teachers present themselves to me. I pray because I am moved by compassion: the compassion of God that I have caught a glimpse of in God's people from time to time.

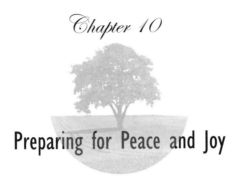

Chapter 10

Preparing for Peace and Joy

Peace and joy may very well be ubiquitous desires. However, while we notice when peace and joy are absent in our lives, we may miss when they are present. In part, this may be true because in order to experience peace and joy, we need a certain mindset. We need to create a certain space to invite peace and joy into our lives. Also, while perhaps peace and joy are often thought of as products, they may be most deeply experienced through the process of living a life filled with meaning, purpose, and hope. The sometimes elusive goal of finding the triad of meaning, purpose, and hope is undoubtedly possible through the process of living a life in an active relationship with the sacred.

There was a recent autumn day when I found myself far from feeling peace and joy. It was a time in my life when I was experiencing a good deal of change, and, with the change, stress. Within a period of a few months my husband and I had our first child, and both had new jobs that moved us to a new city, away from our familiar, loving support system that can be so helpful when taking on the new role of parenting. While the birth of our son and our new jobs were certainly blessings, the transition into our new life came with stress as well.

There was one Saturday morning in particular that I remember sitting with my husband in our kitchen. As was often the case in that point of my life, my thoughts drifted to all that had changed in the recent months. I was thinking about moving away from our friends and family. I was thinking about missing the familiar places and spaces of our old apartment and our old city. I was thinking about the work that lay ahead of me for that day and for that year in my new work role. I was thinking about being a new mom and the challenges of balancing work and family. I was thinking about being overtired, overstressed, and generally overwhelmed. Racing around with the thoughts in my head, I sat at the kitchen table with my husband in silence.

My husband eventually broke that silence. Looking out the kitchen window at the autumn trees, he shared:

"Everything is so pretty."

It was a simple statement said with a gracious inflection. A moment in which he had softly brought his attention to notice the changing leaves outside of our third-floor window. Turning my head, I moved my gaze from within me to outside of me. As I did, for the first time that morning I started to experience the present moment. Thankfully I did, for my husband was right. The trees were spectacular; they were filled with magnificent leaves brilliantly coloring the morning with radiant shades of orange, yellow, gold, and reds.

As we sat longer, I again returned my gaze inward, this time with more intention and purpose. This time my thoughts held more curiosity and awe. In doing so I realized that what I was observing was available to me in this way only in the moment; leaves such as those do not stay long. I also realized that while Matthew and I were sitting at the same kitchen table, living very similar, closely related lives, he was experiencing the morning very differently than I. Because of the perspective he held, peace and joy were close that morning. If not for his comment bringing me toward the experience, too, my thoughts would have only moved me further and further away from the opportunity to experience either.

I started to wonder. How was Matthew meeting life experiences? What was he doing? What was I not doing? What could I learn from Matthew that I was, for some reason, not able to understand on my own? When I deconstruct my husband's perspective in contrast to mine on that fall morning I am aware that we were sitting in the very same moment, the very same space. However, we were sitting so very differently. There were two fundamental qualities of my husband's perspective that my own lacked. Without such qualities the virtues of peace and joy available in that moment for the taking were out of my reach. And they always would be.

My husband met that autumn morning with a sense of mindful appreciation. Mindfulness is a present-moment perspective. While it does not seek to deny or ignore the past or the future, it does not encourage thoughts dwelling in either. Rather, mindfulness seeks to focus on what is available to experience in the present. That Saturday morning, Matthew was not playing a tape in his head, going over a to-do-list of things he wanted to accomplish by tomorrow, or thinking about the yesterday he no longer held. He was fully present in the moment. Thankfully, because he shared his observation, he helped to bring me into the present moment, too. It does not mean he did not miss pieces of our life, as I did. It means he did not allow his appreciation for his past experiences to interfere with his ability to appreciate his present-moment experiences. When mindfulness is coupled with a sense of appreciation, as was present in Matthew's perspective, small things and big things alike are not taken for granted. Ordinary things are experienced for their extraordinariness. One becomes more able to recognize that which is given without even asking, that which is true blessing, that which is undoubtedly a gift from God.

My husband was mindfully appreciative in that Saturday morning moment because he often holds a mindfully appreciative frame. While perhaps there was a time when he practiced mindful appreciation as a way of being in the world, at present he merely intrinsically exists this way. My husband met the autumn leaves with appreciation because it is the way that my husband meets all of the world. It is how he meets others, how he meets himself, and most wonderfully, how he encounters the sacred. There is something intrinsically curious about his stance; he seems to be able to hold a childlike sense of awe. Yet it is coupled with an adult realization of responsibility that we have in the act of seeing. The childlike sense of awe keeps him from falsely believing he has more control than he does in life experiences; the adult realization of his power in the situation keeps him from magically thinking that he has to merely exist and God will do the rest.

Coupled with mindful appreciation, Matthew's perspective was intrinsically sensitive. His perspective allowed him to be affected by what was happening Saturday morning. Matthew's way of being in the world allowed him not only to graciously experience the leaves, but to be moved by them. And it is in this movement that Matthew found the movements of peace and joy, too. His sensitivity, which allowed him to fully honor the external change of the leaves, was also that which allowed him to honor all the changes that he had recently experienced in his life. His sensitivity allowed him to be affected by living in a new city, having a new job, being a new dad. Yet the effect, while perhaps difficult in moments, was positive.

Holding a perspective that nurtures both mindful appreciation and sensitivity helps to create a frame of openness and encourage a sense of calmness. Together they prepare us to experience a lasting sense of peace and joy. Together they frame peace and joy not as an end product but as a process we may tap into in many of life's moments. Peace and joy are not relegated to the extraordinary; they move freely in the ordinary experiences, too. It is up to us to learn to move with them. We so readily talk about peace. We so often seek experiences filled with joy. But they will forever stay in our heads, never to be experienced in our hearts, if we do not seek to live a life that prepares us to experience both.

I don't think my husband specifically sought to experience peace and joy that Saturday morning. If anyone was seeking peace and joy that morning it was surely me. Yet I am certain I would have missed it if not for Matthew. For in that moment when peace and joy felt so far outside of my reach, Matthew's words brought me closer to a perspective that encourages my ability to experience both. Matthew lives life in a way that encourages me to not miss life. He encourages me to not miss myself, to not miss others, and not to miss moments to appreciate God. Matthew lives life in a way that proclaims that we are processes, not products. We are ever in the making. And so are the virtues that we may experience. Peace and joy are processes filled with a motion that, if understood and then nurtured, can serve to inspire us to not merely live a life, but to live one that flourishes.

Chapter 11

Fostering a Sense of Gratitude

The parish I worked in was a vibrant combination of students and community members. While the two groups could easily become isolated entities, purposeful effort was made to integrate the students and community members in meaningful ways. One such way was a long tradition of preparing a home-cooked meal in the church hall for students after the five o'clock Sunday evening liturgy. Over the years I grew to understand that students came to the Sunday student suppers for many reasons. They came because it was free. They came because it was an alternative to the dining hall. They came for the fellowship among students and with other parishioners, many of whom worked for the university as faculty or staff. They came searching for an experience less like school and more like home.

It was at a student supper where I first met Crescentia. She had been a volunteer in the program for all of her adult life. For her, cooking and serving student suppers was a family affair. Her mother, father, and two daughters volunteered together. All the parishioners who volunteered were wonderful. They all cared about bridging the disconnection between the students and the community. All the parishioners who volunteered were invested in the experience. All of the volunteers worked hard, oftentimes cooking for close to seventy-five people.

Yet there was something extra-memorable about Crescentia. She had a way, by virtue of her presence, of welcoming people. She was charismatic, energetic, and confident. These three qualities were accompanied by a deep sense of gratitude that allowed her charisma not to blind her sincerity, her energy not to envelop her intentionality, and her confidence not to cover her humility. By sitting with Crescentia one was able, perhaps more than any other volunteer I met, to—for a moment—come to forget that they were eating in a large church hall and believe they were in the comforts of Crescentia's home. Crescentia was an example of Sunday student suppers at their best. Sitting with Crescentia, one got the sense that it was less of a concern to satisfy a hungry stomach, and more of a concern to satisfy a hungry soul—one that longed to believe that people fundamentally were good. Crescentia could affirm such a search.

With such an honest presence, it was obvious when Crescentia became sick. Not because she was any less engaging. Not because she missed serving a Sunday meal at her turn. I don't recall that she ever did. But because you notice when people you care about are at war. Crescentia's battle was with breast cancer. And for a long time, she was winning. And for a long time, she allowed us to watch her win. We were a better community of people for it.

Crescentia developed breast cancer when her daughters were just entering adolescence. Her family was optimistic; her doctors were optimistic; we as her church community were optimistic. Cancer took Crescentia's hair. But she did not let it take her heart. Cancer tried to consume her, but she would not let it. She fought the illness with all that she was, not only for her own sake but for the sake of her family. Most especially it seemed she fought for the sake of her still young daughters. And things turned around. Crescentia improved. Crescentia was, for a time, cancer-free.

As it seems to be with extraordinary people, a return to baseline functioning, to live as it were before cancer, was not good enough for Crescentia. Her struggle had allowed her insight to the existential questions that children, such as her own, struggle with when a parent develops cancer. Crescentia recognized that while life's ultimate questions are difficult to answer as adults, they are even more challenging for a child to hold as they are still in the process of developing a coherent sense of self in the world. Along with insight, Crescentia was also filled with gratitude after her recovery. As such, she was inspired to help other families who were experiencing a similar struggle. With the support and encouragement of family and friends, Crescentia eventually started work on a nonprofit organization that provides an adventure-based group experience for children whose parents were diagnosed with cancer. The experience helps children reclaim a sense of control, to feel less alone, and at least equally as important, to have some fun. My mother-in-law, Anne Werdel, a wise friend and mother herself of five children, said once to me that in a successful family, you always tend to "lean in the direction of the most vulnerable person or people at the time." And I think this is what Crescentia was doing by starting her nonprofit. Crescentia was the one who was sick, but she recognized that her children, and children of other parents with cancer, are in many ways still the most vulnerable. So she leaned toward her children and created a way for other parents to lean toward their own.

In her sickness and in her recovery, Crescentia was inspiring the whole church community. It seemed to me that she was ever more helpful, ever more loving, and ever more loved by the parishioners, students, and community members alike. Of course, the degree to which we inspire people, help people, and love people does not protect us from struggle and pain entering our lives. How well we fight one battle does not necessarily keep a second battle at bay. Sadly, this was the case for Crescentia.

Having moved to work on my doctoral studies, I was no longer working at the church when Crescentia's cancer returned. Still I kept in touch with many parishioners. I heard from many people, including Crescentia's mother, that this time the experience of cancer was different. It was more threatening, more powerful. The treatments were more painful, more trying, more experimental. Crescentia's doctors demonstrated less optimism. This time Crescentia seemed to have less fight in her.

Every now and again when I would return to the church for Mass, there were many people I hoped to see there. Crescentia was always one of them. The last time I saw Crescentia was at a Thanksgiving Eve Mass, a service to give thanks to God for the blessings received that year. It was a place and space where people came to feel and perhaps find gratitude. Crescentia was there.

She was sitting three pews in front of me. Yet even from the distance, I could tell Crescentia was noticeably weakened. She was sitting with her father, whose weary expression said all I needed to know. Crescentia was not winning this battle with cancer. Crescentia was dying.

During the sign of the peace, Crescentia exited her pew and moved slowly toward me. I remember she gave me a hug.

I remember her feeling frail. I remember her saying that it was good to see me. Taken aback by her weakness, I remember I could only smile and return a hug. I remember not having words for all that I wanted to say. I remember her returning to her pew. I remember her walking away. I remember praying. I prayed with great sadness in my heart for fear that this would be the last time I ever saw Crescentia. And I prayed with deep gratitude on that Thanksgiving Eve for being someone Crescentia was grateful to see. I prayed to understand better the faith that allowed someone in such a state to still hold gratitude.

A few months later, I learned that Crescentia had died. Hundreds of people attended her funeral, coming from literally all over the world to be in the presence of each other in the hopes of reclaiming a bit of Crescentia. After the service there was a reception in the church hall—the same hall that held the student suppers—the same hall where I first met Crescentia.

I have stayed in touch with her mother years after her death. Over one cup of coffee Crescentia's mother gave me a copy of Crescentia's oldest daughter's college essay. I remember putting it in my purse to read at a later time. I knew it would be about her mother. When I was home and all was quiet, in the early evening, I opened the essay. In it, the story of Crescentia was presented from her daughter's perspective. The essay spoke of many things. It spoke of love, of struggle, of triumph, of loss, of pain, and of redemption. Most profoundly, the essay spoke of gratitude.

With full acknowledgment of the profound loss that she experienced, Crescentia's daughter wrote of how her mother had taught her that life is a gift never to be taken for granted. She wrote of how her mother had taught her to appreciate life and to work through suffering and pain: the physical pain of cancer and the emotional pain of separation. She wrote of her gratitude for the perspective that she now held close. Crescentia lived an extraordinary, grateful life and her spirit was alive now in her daughter's voice, in her daughter's life. And because I was privileged enough to read the essay and to know Crescentia, the inspiration to live an extraordinary, grateful life was now alive in me, too.

Crescentia knew well that this life was a gift and that while it was the end of her journey, it was not the end of her daughter's. So in her life and in her death she found a way to encourage them. In her life and in her death, though I doubt she realized it, she found a way to encourage me, too. These are the words I wish I had spoken to Crescentia in our last interaction. If I could have another chance to speak to her, I would tell her thank you. While I missed that opportunity then, I earnestly try to say thank you now both quietly in my prayers and loudly with my life. I do so that I may not merely move forward in life, but so that I may have the courage, the strength, and the perspective to move forward well.

Chapter 12

Maintaining Spiritual Strength

A while back I had a conversation with a young adult about God. He asked me numerous questions about faith. Some questions were complex, some were simple, and many were somewhere in between. Of all the questions he asked, however, one seemed to be at the heart of his wondering: "Do you feel a connection with God?" When I acknowledged that I did, he shared his belief that such an experience was both unusual and amazing for a young adult. As we talked longer, it became clear that there were indeed moments in his life when he felt close to the sacred. Most notably, he felt a meaningful, comforting connection with God at his grandmother's funeral. He imagined, too, that he would feel a more meaningful connection with God in the future, when he approached the end of his life. Yet beyond the extraordinary moments of life and death, God remained more of an elusive idea. Every day he experienced faith as more of a hope than as a belief. He spoke with a sense of awe when considering the possibility of a constant connection to God as a way of being that could actually be true.

The sincerity with which he was asking questions about faith encouraged me to ask one important question of my own. I began to wonder why one person can take momentary experiences of God and weave them into a meaningful relationship with the sacred while others allow them to be experienced as exceptions in one's relationship with God. If a meaningful connection with God had been experienced in the past, if an encounter with the sacred had been experienced before, then what does a person need in place in order to remain connected to God in the many more ordinary moments that make up the bulk of our life?

I started to consider my own erratic movements of faith. In doing so, I kept returning to the word *relationship* and an understanding that relationships always start with an awareness of the other. For instance, I know when I am losing God. I can hear in my voice when my relationship with God is slipping away. I start to think of myself as beginning and end, losing any sort of perspective beyond me. I can see it in my motion when I am disconnecting from my relationship with the sacred. I lose stillness. I feel as though I have no center. My movements become less purposeful and more chaotic. I carry a feeling of being underwhelmed in the ordinary experiences of life. Meaning and purpose can start to feel absent.

I also know when I feel a connection with God. I find myself thinking beyond myself, considering the ways that I relate to others, both those who it is easy to be close with and those whose closeness causes me a significant amount of distress. I can easily find stillness and silence in my days. It feels natural to remain curious and full of wonder. I readily recognize the spiritual questions intrinsic in everyday life experiences. Regardless of whether in a moment God feels close or a bit further away, regardless if God feels like a dear friend or complete mystery, when I have a connection with God I always feel as though I can locate the sacred. I have access to him. He is available to me. Our relationship is strong, and consequently I feel spiritually strong.

There are a few things I purposefully do that help the relationship remain strong. It starts with intentionally creating space for my relationship with God. Rather than leaving my relationship to fight for itself, I fight for it. I do this by valuing it, tending to it, protecting it from the people and things in life that may lead me away from it, deny its worthiness, or question its usefulness. I go out of my way to honor the space where I may encounter the sacred.

In this sacred space, I seek God in my prayer. Valuing my relationship with God means I need to value prayer that is both honest and sincere. I have seen in my own life how if I begin to feel detached from the words I pray, then my relationship with God begins to feel detached as well. Yet when my prayer comes from the deepest part of my being, my relationship with God feels rooted in the same deep place. When my prayer comes from the deepest, most honest part of me, I experience prayer not only as the intentional way in which I turn toward God but it feels as though, in prayer, God also turns toward me. My lips and heart are not giving a speech; they are having a conversation. Our conversation can take many forms. If one form begins to feel distant, I have the ability to search for another form. When and if I become frustrated in my prayer, I try not to run from it. Rather, I seek ways to lean further into it. I give my prayer more attention rather than less.

While much of my prayer life feels private, I recognize that to remain strong in my relationship with God, I cannot always be in isolation. I need to hear not only my voice but the voice of a community. I need others' conversations. I need others' questions. I need others' proclamations. I need others' testimonials. I need their eyes, hearts, and minds. I need their tears. I need to selflessly wonder about them, and I need them to compassionately wonder about me. Why? Because I do not believe that I have enough wisdom of my own for this journey. So then I need to hear, share, and create wisdom in communion with others. Alone, the most I can hope for is to understand the God who lives in me. But only in communion can I understand the God who lives in us. And it is with this dynamic, complex God that I seek a meaningful relationship.

For many reasons we tend to forget—or perhaps some live life never fully understanding—that while we often talk about relationships as products, they are really processes. Successful mothers do not mother every once in a while; they are constantly mothering. Successful marriages are not dictated by the attention paid to the wedding day, but the everyday. If relationships are to flourish (which is often the implicit goal when one enters a relationship), they cannot merely be claimed once. They must be found over and over again as we move about our days, weeks, months, years, and lives. This type of availability demands a constant source of energy. For without the energy to attend, even the most wonderful and natural relationships can begin to feel unusual and uncomfortable. Even the closest of friends can become strangers with distance and time.

This is also true in considering one's relationship with God. We do not find God once; we continue to find him. We don't understand him once; we are constantly coming to understand him. The key in maintaining an adult spirituality is to adopt practices that keep one spiritually strong so that one has the wherewithal to continue to turn his attention toward God each day. This enables one to live life looking back with belief, forward with hope, and be fully alive in the present moment to experience God. Then our lives may not become fragmented experiences of the sacred, but rather one long, beautiful conversation with God.

Chapter 13

The Journey Ahead

My time as a campus minister came to a close with a decision to move to Honduras. I had been to Honduras three times before with groups of students on spring-break trips. My next trip would be alone, for an undetermined amount of time, and in a new part of the country. With such a great transition fast approaching, my mind was often filled with excitement and concern for my journey ahead.

I wanted to go to Honduras for many reasons, not the least of which was the children. There were many children whose stories and faces had left their imprints on my heart, and I wanted more—more time, more connections, more understanding. Perhaps no one left a larger imprint than a small-framed, brown-haired girl of six years old named Gabriela. I came to know Gabriela on my first of a dozen trips to a Quiscamote, a small, impoverished farming community in the mountains of Honduras. As I stood at the entrance of the town attempting to quietly and intellectually make sense of the extreme poverty before my eyes, Gabriela, without me immediately realizing, placed her small hand into mine. With just the few steps that Gabriela and I walked together, she gently touched a piece of my heart.

I came to learn that Gabriela lived with no electricity, no running water, and little food. She spoke incessantly to me on the first trip. Though I spoke not a word of Spanish at the time, she insisted that I understood her; on some level, I suppose I did. For what Gabriela was explaining to me did not need words. I came to learn from Gabriela that one does not need many external commonalities to nurture a spiritual life. My encounters with God are universally open for all.

With time and language school I learned Spanish. On the trip prior to my last, I had a real conversation with Gabriela; I asked her many questions. She touched my hair, admiring the different shades of blonde and brown; she wondered out loud how my hair could be so many different colors at once. Many times she took my hand to compare the shades of our skin. She looked at me as if to ask, "But how can this be that we look so different?" She asked me how I made my eyes blue. I asked her what she needed, imagining a laundry list of articles. I had decided in my heart that I would not ask such a questions if I was not prepared to find ways to respond. She took a great deal of time to reflect upon the question, so long I wondered if perhaps my Spanish was incomprehensible. She eventually answered quietly, perhaps as any six-year-old anywhere in the world would: "María, necesito una muñeca," meaning, "Mary, I need a doll."

Later that evening, Gabriela's mother invited me to her house to share a cup of coffee. With no electricity in the village, I went to visit her home wearing a headlamp. The light became the entertainment and conversation piece of the evening. Gabriela's father and some of the other men at the house that night took turns trying on the headlamp. Gabriela climbed into my lap as if she had known me her whole life. She spoke to me as if we always were friends and I never would leave. I see now how Gabriela, in her encounter with me, was modeling how I want to encounter God; Gabriela was modeling how I now believe God encounters me.

When I did leave Quiscamote, I left my headlamp, along with any lingering belief that the small "we" of Gabriela and me and the large "we" of anybody and everyone else are not divinely connected. Months later, back in the States, I found a doll that resembled Gabriela. I sent it to her with a friend of mine who was traveling to the village and attached a note that read, "Gabriela, I pray that God takes care of our friendship. I pray that He takes care of you." And I anticipated the day that I would return to Quiscamote and to Gabriela.

Even with such a deep desire to return to Honduras, I found myself filled with a sense of loneliness about my journey ahead. I felt a need to disconnect from the part of the world that I was living in and at the same time I felt an inability to fully connect yet to the part of world I would for a short, undetermined amount of time call home.

One of places where I found myself thinking about my upcoming journey to Honduras and my sense of loneliness was on some of my last volunteer trips to a local children's home that was a very large part of my life. My work as campus minister included establishing a volunteer program between the children's home and the university students at the church. When the program started, I would accompany the volunteers on all the trips. There were weeks when it felt as if I was at the children's home more than I was on campus. As the program developed, my visits were only once a week. As my trip to

Honduras grew closer, my time in the United States, and thus at the children's home, was drawing to a close.

The idea of leaving my connection with the home was very sad for me, as the home was a very special place. It is cared for by a small group of Catholic nuns. They are indeed the most prayerful and patient women I have ever met. It was easy to see why the children loved living at the home, even in this most difficult time in their life; the sisters shared a deep and healing love with children and volunteers alike.

As a volunteer I learned that all the children in the home were removed from their previous homes because of court-found cases of abuse or neglect. I learned as well that the primary hope for the children was to be reunited with parents. The courts gave a certain amount of time for the parents to demonstrate their changed behavior. And so the result was that the children lived in a land of limbo—not yet able to be placed in foster homes or adoption situations, and not yet able to be reunited with their birth parent or parents. When parents appealed for more time from the courts, the children spent more time in limbo at the home. In the four years I was there, I noticed that some children were reunited quickly; others were placed in foster homes quickly. Some of the children stayed at the home far longer than others. Sara was one of the girls who lived at the children's home for almost the entire four years that I volunteered.

As a volunteer, I did not know Sara's whole story. I knew only that she was living at the children's home because she had been removed from her parents because of severe parental abuse, that she had lived at the home for at least three and a half years, and that she had not yet told me she had a "new home," as the children often did months before they would actually leave. I also knew, from the volunteer training, that the older the child grew the more difficult it was for the state to find an adoption placement. Foster care was still a possible option, but having a "new mom and dad," as the children would come to dream, grew more difficult with age.

I remember one afternoon at the home, toward the end of my volunteering. I was in the front yard playing with some of the children when there appeared in the sky a very large rainbow. It was truly amazing to see. Perhaps no one was as amazed, as in awe, or as excited as Sara, who at the time was around nine years old. Sara was so filled with excitement that she had to tell someone. So she shouted, in a very loud voice across the front yard for the attention of one of the caretakers. "Sister, Sister! So you see it! Do you see it! Do you see the R-A-I-N-B-O-W!" The word rainbow fell slowly and purposefully from her lips.

It would have been difficult not to hear Sara. She was so loud, so excited, and so physically far away from the caretaker whose attention she was calling.

The very gentle and aware sister replied in a calm and stable voice. "Yes, Sara, I see the rainbow."

But Sara wanted more, so she continued. "Do you know what that means?! Do you know what that means, Sister? The RAINBOW!"

I continued to listen, as often I gained bits of wisdom from the sister's way of responding to questions that I would often attempt to mimic with the children in my own interactions. As well, Sara had hooked me with her excitement about the rainbow. I found myself smiling as I watched Sara barely able to contain her own content. I wondered what she would do with all that energy.

Before the sister could even start to consider how she would respond, Sara was speaking again. She exclaimed, "The rainbow means that God will not leave us orphaned! That's what it means, sister."

I don't even know what the sister said, if she said anything at all. For with this phrase, proudly proclaimed from the mouth of a little girl who very well could be orphaned for the rest of her life, God once again broke open my heart and filled me with all the pain and sadness of Sara and all of her deep hope and joy.

And I held it then in that moment in Sara's front yard, and when I am mindfully in prayer, I can hold it still.

I don't know if Sara realized how profound a statement she had made. But I guess profound statements aren't really for the people who make them. Sara's voice was the voice of God, and it was speaking right to me. He would not leave this beautiful girl alone, and neither would he leave me alone in my journey ahead. My eyes filled with tears—for Sara and her dream of a loving family, for Gabriela and her innocent request for a doll, and for me and for the good-byes and hellos that lay ahead. And in all my actions, in all my encounters, in all my ways of being and knowing, what it means to be a person seeking a relationship with the sacred, I try to emulate this experience with Sara. I attempt to break open life's little epiphanies by allowing them to break me open. I believe that if our goal is to thrive by living a life in deep relationship with the sacred, we should all become more open to these moments of grace when God speaks unexpectedly through the mouths of babes and others in our lives.

Maturing spirituality is learning how to stare in awe at this world with the heart of a child, to understand this world with the mind of a sage, and to speak clearly to this world with the voice of a prophet. All of this so that we may see that all of life, just as all lives—those deeply broken and those deeply blessed—are ways of encountering God.

Chapter 14

Universal Connections and Unique Truths

Our relationship with God is unique to us. This, in part, is what makes it so wonderful. While others may pray to the same God, perhaps even the same prayers, perhaps even at the same time, our God answers us individually. He calls us each by name. Yet, without dishonoring the uniqueness, there is of course a common thread that weaves us together and so weaves together our experiences of God. In relationship with God, as we come to more deeply know the unique truths of ourselves, we are pulled more and more out of ourselves and into an understanding of our connection with others. Throughout the stories presented in this book, and the many more throughout each of our lives, spirituality continues to reveal itself to be the delicate and durable something that holds us together.

The delicateness of spirituality can be seen by virtue of how easily, how readily, how often we miss the sacred in our lives. Softly, simply, gently, God exists in the moments of our lives. We may come to deepen our relationship with God if we can find a way to exist softly, simply, and gently there, too. An infant's smile, the melody of a song, the rising and setting of the sun and many other such moments all invite us to live sensitively present in each moment with God.

However, for many reasons and much of the time, many of us live very far from ourselves. Consequently, we live very far from our delicate God. In turn we risk losing sight of how we belong to God and each other. Treating ourselves and others kindly, taking time to experience the communal experience of Mass, living in relationship with the poor and oppressed, fostering a sense of openness in our image of self, and inviting the still, small voice of God and others to enter our lives will all serve to bring us gracefully together.

Fortunately for us who often struggle to be thoughtfully present in our lives, spirituality reveals itself to be quite durable, too. Regardless of whether we acknowledged him in the past, regardless of whether we will acknowledge him in the future, God never fails to endure. And so the opportunity to encounter the sacred may pass, but it never passes for long. A relationship with God can be ignored, overlooked, and untapped, but it remains always available. A relationship with the sacred will always be with and part of us through whatever life brings, for as long as our life lasts.

When it is honored and nurtured, we come to find that spirituality is hard-wearing. It can bear first breaths and last breaths. It remains present when anniversaries are celebrations with those we hold dear, and when they are days of remembrance of the ones we can no longer hold. Spirituality continues through it all. Even more miraculously, sometimes not in spite of, but because of what we are asked to endure, our spirituality can even grow. In the often slow and shaky process of coming to own our spiritual heritage, in the difficult, sometimes painful path of growth toward wisdom, and in coming to find the process of peace and joy, we may grow more deeply into God. While we may dismiss it for a lengthy period of time or call upon it in every instance of our life, we can't wear spirituality out, as we do a piece of cloth. It will forever be part of each of us. It will always be holding us, weaving us, keeping us together as only our durable God can.

In my work I came to meet a woman whose child, Emily, died of leukemia at the age of eleven. It was a profoundly difficult loss. A single mom, Emily was her only child. There were so many questions that Emily's mother could not answer, and so much of the time she was overwhelmed with a sense of unrest. She was understandably sad and lonely. She was understandably seeking to comprehend a world, an existence without Emily.

There were a number of triggers during the day that caused her to cognitively stop in her tracks. The one that seemed most paralyzing was when the word lost was used in common expressions. If a person casually mentioned that she lost her keys, or if perhaps it slipped off her own tongue in the same manner, she was immediately pulled out of her present activity, and into the moment when she watched her daughter take her last breath as she lovingly, stroked her daughter's head as only a mother could.

At midnight, on what would have been her daughter's twelfth birthday, in bright red erasable marker, she wrote on the dry erase board on the refrigerator a note, a proclamation, a plea, a prayer, a cry. Her mother's pain, her sadness, her longing, her love were all wrapped up in seven simple words:

HAPPY BIRTHDAY, EMILY.
I LOVE YOU.
MOM

Emily's mother's story, her words, and her feelings resonated deeply with me. I was not myself a mother at the time nor did I need to be to feel our connection. My own story of loss, of hope for a reunion, and of pain at the realization that such a reunion would not be on this earth came to me; in this time, in this place, loss reminds us that we cannot always be satiated in the ways that we so desperately want. I came to understand that to be with Emily's mother fully, I needed to honor her story, her loss, her life, and as her own personal journey. By acknowledging Emily's mother's story, I was able to see how our stories were deeply connected. Though the actual moments were different, we experienced the same sense of loss as well as some of the same longings. We understood the same experience of an emptiness that could no longer be filled, of a space that would forever be open. We asked the same existential questions. We were both human, praying to the same great God for compassion, comfort, comprehension, and companionship.

Yet the more I sat with Emily's mother, the more I understood that our connection was not rooted in despair. We were connected by something greater than us, and something greater than loss. With time I came to realize that the deep connection I felt was not our loss but our human experiences and drive for the divine. Connection is not about having the same human experience as another. It is about seeing each other as part of the same human experience, seeing each other and ourselves in the image and likeness of the divine. It is about continuing to ask myself as I engage with people in this world, if I truly believe that we are part of the same story. And in faith, it is then about living the response.

As this book attempts to highlight, we need to consider the way we are living. We need to consider how we answer spiritual questions in the way we live our lives. This book has been about sharing the experiential ways in which I have noticed in my life how people answer the spiritual questions:

Do I belong to God?
Do I own my faith?
Who do I believe is responsible for my faith development?
What is my relationship with the poor?
Do I notice the injustice that exists?
Do I value stillness and silence?
Do I hide my pain?
Do I believe in peace and joy?
Do I live a grateful life?
How do I hold the sacred?
How do I limit or restrict God?
Are we connected to each other's stories?
What do we hold as truth?

As our faith matures and we begin to consider how we answer such questions with our lives, we may come to see that there was always a piece of us that already knew that we are spiritual beings. There was always a piece of us already knowing, already crying, already longing for God. There has always been a place within us that understands that we belong to God.

We can and will grow in our faith when we see how natural it is to take God beyond Sunday and come to own our spirituality. We will do this by finding space for silence, preparing our hearts for peace and joy, nurturing a sense of gratitude, starting to see and seek God, and learning to hold the universal truth that God is always within and among us. He always has been and always will be. In each of our lives and among all of our stories, in the inhalation and exhalation of each breath—God is always with us. As we come to know this, we can better prepare our ears to hear and our eyes to see how everything broken, everything blessed, and in everything, everywhere that we find ourselves, there is a question to be fully asked, an opportunity with our life to answer it, and a chance to deepen our experience with the sacred. In every moment, God is inviting us to embrace the spiritual questions that we hold, to walk courageously with him, and to own our life which by design is intrinsically and beautifully spiritual. Knowing this, what more could we ever be waiting for?

Appendices

The following appendices have been provided for those who have finished reading this experiential book and would like to take time to reflect with the material in a slower, more deliberate way.

The first appendix is a list of fourteen elements of an adult spirituality. The second appendix is a series of fourteen short meditations. Both the elements and the actions correspond with the themes of each chapter in this book. The elements and meditations may be reviewed on your own or with a group of your peers who may be seeking a more intentional and mature relationship with God as well. However they are used, my hope is that the appendices can serve as a means to further encourage a deeper, closer, and more constant connection to the sacred for those who desire it.

Faith is certainly a journey. Therefore, while these reflections and meditations may be useful to some degree the first time through, they can also most certainly be returned to again and again as a person feels the need for support, structure, or encouragement along the way.

Appendix I

A person who seeks to live life by engaging and nurturing a personal relationship with the sacred purposefully attempts to:

1. Vision oneself as connected to God.

2. Own one's faith experience and faith journey.

3. Think and live with a social-justice-minded heart.

4. Carve out quiet space daily for meditation and prayer.

5. Journey through the multitude of life's daily activities with a sense of centeredness.

6. Hold brokenness and blessings together as one.

7. Live life with the understanding that our time is finite, and that we are making a journey toward our eternal home.

8. See the self and others with kind, gentle eyes.

9. Work to gain awareness of one's spiritual giftedness and one's spiritual limitations. With awareness one then works to soften the spiritual shadow that they now recognize as part of them.

10. Practice being mindfully appreciative and sensitive to experiences of God.

11. Foster a sense of gratitude for all of life's gifts.

12. Place value on one's relationship with God in heart, mind, and through all actions.

13. Live in the moment while journeying toward a deeper sense of home.

14. Search for the universal connections that intertwine an individual life story with those of others.

1. Consider the connections and disconnections that exist between your image of self and your image of God.

2. Be thankful for the tradition that has been handed to you while wondering about how close or far you feel from owning your faith.

3. Be open to experiences of God in your own interactions with those in need and be open to your own neediness.

4. Create some quiet space and time in your life so you may hear God whisper words of love.

5. Practice being still and become open to what you may come to understand about your relationship with God in doing so.

6. Consider how you have witnessed the paradox of brokenness and blessings as part of the human experience.

7. Take time to reflect upon the finiteness of this life and consider the ways that understanding this may change the way you choose to live.

8. Practice seeing yourself and others with kinder, gentler eyes, incorporating into your perspective a balanced understanding of the relationship between your strengths and your imperfections.

9. Remind yourself of the connection between your spiritual gifts and your spiritual growth.

10. Hold on to your childlike sense of awe as you work toward an adult acceptance of the responsibility you have in your faith experience. As you do you may grow ever more mindfully appreciative of and sensitively attuned to that which is a gift in this world.

11. Living a grateful life may begin by daily considering and even listing all that you have been blessed with in your life.

12. Consider creating space, leaning into your prayer, and gathering in community as ways to continually rediscover the mystery of God in your life.

13. Allow yourself to be broken open by little moments of life so that you may grow in an understanding of the ways in which God experiences life with you.

14. Grow in awareness of how the questions you hold about life are often answered even before you ask them by the way you live your life.

Suggested Reading List for Deepening One's Experiences of God

The aim of this book is to introduce the reader to the experience of knowing God. We may each live life answering questions that we have yet to fully (or ever) ask. For those who have a desire to read further on themes that have been identified in this book on an experiential level, the following short suggested reading list is provided. This is by no means an exhaustive list. Rather, it is a starting point for the readers who are interested in continuing to deepen their experiences of God.

Sister Joan Chittister (2011). *The Monastery of the Heart: An Invitation to a Meaningful Life.* Bluebridge: Katonah, NY.

Sister Joan Chittister (2012). *Following the Path: The Search for a Life of Passion, Purpose, and Joy.* Image Books: New York.

Tilden Edwards (1995). *Living in the Presence: Spiritual Exercises to Open Our Lives to the Awareness of God.* HarperOne: New York.

Thomas Keating (2009). *Intimacy with God: An Introduction to Centering Prayer.* Crossroad: Chestnut Ridge, NY.

Thomas Keating (1994). *Open Mind Open Heart: The Contemplative Dimension of the Gospel.* Continuum: New York.

Thomas Merton (1971). *Contemplative Prayer.* Image Books: New York.

Thomas Merton (1999). *Thoughts in Solitude.* Farrar, Straum, and Giroux: New York.

Henri J.M. Nouwen (1981). *Making All Things New: An Invitation to the Spiritual Life.* HarperOne: San Francisco.

Henri J.M. Nouwen (2006). *Here and Now: Living in the Spirit*, 10th edition. Crossroad: Chestnut Ridge, NY.

Henri J.M. Nouwen (1991). *The Way of the Heart: The Spirituality of the Desert Fathers and Mothers.* HarperOne: San Francisco.

Parker J. Palmer (1999). *Let Your Life Speak: Listening for the Voice of Vocation.* Jossey-Bass: San Francisco.

Karl Rahner (1999). *Encounters With Silence.* St. Augustine's Press: South Bend, IN.

Richard Rohr (2003). *Everything Belongs: The Gift of Contemplative Prayer.* Crossroad: Chestnut Ridge, NY.

Joyce Rupp (2008). *Open the Door: A Journey to the True Self.* Ave Maria Press: Notre Dame, IN.

Robert J. Wicks (2000). *Everyday Simplicity: A Practical Guide to Spiritual Growth.* Sorin: Notre Dame, IN.

Robert J. Wicks (2012). *Riding the Dragon: 10 Lessons for Inner Strength in Challenging Times.* Sorin: Notre Dame, IN.

How Can I Find God?
The Famous and the Not-So-Famous Consider the Quintessential Question

ISBN: 978-0-7648-0090-0

This vibrant collection brings together an array of voices addressing the question of how one might approach the search for God. With contributors from many faith traditions, this book will be of value to all who seek to answer the question, "How Can I Find God?"

Spiritual Blueprint
How We Live, Work, Love, Play, and Pray

ISBN: 978-0-7648-1892-9

Spiritual Blueprint helps you simplify your life, reduce stress, and understand your higher purpose by taking inventory and rebuilding the five "homes" of your life: Body, Hands, Heart, Mind, and Spirit. An integrated workbook walks you through the steps to identifying your strengths and weaknesses.

Handbook for Today's Catholic – Revised Edition
ISBN: 978-0-7648-1220-0

Handbook for Today's Catholic is presented in easy-to-understand language, with content divided into Beliefs, Practices, Prayers, and Living the Faith, and is fully indexed to the *Catechism of the Catholic Church*. RCIA and parish adult faith formation groups, high school religious education classes, inquirers into the Catholic Faith, and people who want to have the essentials of Catholicism at their fingertips will welcome this affordable faith resource.